D0098647

The Prisoners of Perote

Barker Texas History Center Series, No. 1

The Prisoners of Perote

Containing a Journal Kept by the Author,
Who Was Captured by the Mexicans, at Mier,
December 25, 1842, and Released
from Perote, May 16, 1844

by William Preston Stapp

Illustrations by Charles Shaw

University of Texas Press   Austin & London

Library of Congress Cataloging in Publication Data

Stapp, William Preston.
The prisoners of Perote.

(Barker Texas History Center series, no. 1)
Reprint of the 1845 ed. published by G. B. Zieber,
Philadelphia; with new foreword.
1. Mier Expedition, 1842–Personal narratives.
2. Stapp, William Preston. 3. Texas–Militia–Biography.
4. Soldiers–Texas–Biography. 5. Mexico–Description
and travel. I. Title. II. Series: Eugene C.
Barker Texas History Center. Barker Texas History Center
Series, no. 1.
F390.S79 1977 976.4'04'0924 77-22425
ISBN 0-292-76442-1

Foreword and illustrations copyright © 1977
by the University of Texas Press

Printed in the United States of America

This edition is reset from the publication by
G. B. Zieber and Company, Philadelphia, 1845

TO GENERAL MILTON STAPP,

Madison, Indiana.

Sir,–

Your kindness in administering to my necessities, while a prisoner in Mexico, and the assiduity with which you prosecuted your application for my release from that imprisonment, and your final success in procuring my liberty, deserves, as it has received, the highest reward that a grateful heart can give. And your friendship to me shall be held in grateful recollection to the latest hour of my life. More than this, I have not in my power to bestow, except it be to give you a faithful history of that eventful period of my life; which you will find in the following pages, and which is here most respectfully inscribed to you, by one who is proud to acknowledge you as his friend, and most earnestly desires that your life may be long, happy, and useful.

I am Sir,

Yours, with great respect,

WILLIAM P. STAPP.

Contents

BOOK II

xiii

Foreword

If there is an inscription over the portal leading into Perote prison, it should have been copied directly from the pedestal on which the Goddess of Liberty stands in New York harbor:

> Give me your tired, your poor,
> Your huddled masses yearning to breathe free,
> The wretched refuse of your teeming shore.

For Emma Lazarus' lines fit the several batches of prisoners who walked from Texas to Perote. Whatever they were back home, they wound up in Mexico, wretched, huddled, and yearning to be free. Perote was no "golden door" beside which a Goddess of Liberty could lift her lamp. But it was a refuge of sorts into which Texans from the Republic of Texas were herded almost with regularity. Here came prisoners from the abortive Texan Santa Fe Expedition, from the Nicholas Dawson Expedition, and from the Mier Expedition. I doubt that anyone ever took a careful census of the number of Texans in Perote at the same time, but between the winter of 1841–1842 and sometime in 1843, altogether about 550 Texans were gathered within the confines of this forbidding prison. With today's population explosion in Mexico the town of Perote still checks out at less than 10,000 *ciudadanos*, and in the 1840's it must have been correspondingly smaller. If the Texans had been permitted to bloc vote, which of course they weren't, they could undoubtedly have held the balance of power in the town's municipal elections.

Nowadays Perote does not look particularly forbidding. On a secondary highway from Veracruz to Puebla, it lies just 30 kilometers upland from the provincial capital of Jalapa, a most civilized city. Its altitude would probably measure at about 7,000 feet, its climate is invariably temperate if a bit windy, and the nearby flora is a bit on the orchidaceous side. It barely misses being a gardenia spot that sits on the dry side of the dividing line between the damp coastland and the vast central valley of Mexico.

But Texans of the 1840's had no appreciation for the pleasures of Perote, any more than prisoners a half-century later enjoyed terri-

torial prison at Yuma because of its parallel opportunities for sun-
bathing. Men yearning to be free don't care for incarceration, and
complaints emanating from within Perote's thick, damp walls were
bitter and unceasing.

Perote Castle had been built by the Spanish authorities between
1769 and 1775—about the time that the American independence
movement was preparing to burst loose. It had two aims: to guard a
principal trade route from the coast to Mexico City and to serve as a
depository for treasure awaiting shipment to Spain. The fortress itself was rather routine, as Spanish fortresses go. It covered approximately 26 acres and had a moat around its inner walls. When the
Mexicans replaced the Spanish, they transformed Perote into a prison. By the time the Texans arrived, the building was more than 70
years old, an antique by upstart Texas standards. And given the
probable repair climate in Mexico, which for a third of a century had
been more concerned with politics and fighting than with upkeep,
Perote was undoubtedly in miserable shape.

In some ways conditions in Perote seemed to have paralleled conditions in Texas when that entity flew the Mexican flag. The Mexican captors were extraordinarily generous, permitting prisoners to
write and receive letters from home, evidently without censorship;
to receive visitors, money, and gifts; and to wander into town to
purchase supplies. The opportunity for shopping was undoubtedly
limited; in Perote today, opportunity for purchasing remains limited, despite the omnipresent Coca-Cola and Sears Roebuck products. Although international law was not as advanced then as now,
Texans had an elevated idea of what it meant to be prisoners of war,
and consequently chafed because the Mexicans forced them to perform common labor. Possibly the activity involved saved them from
that most besetting of all woes in a prison environment, boredom,
but the Texans detested any evidence of overlordship.

On the other hand, the Mexicans resented the fact that the Texans
had insulted the integrity of Mexican institutions by coming on
their soil to fight and to dissect the territory. Since no declared war
existed, they hardly viewed the Texans as prisoners of war. The fair-
skinned men from the north and east were just plain invaders, *ban-
ditos*. The observance of international law then becomes a matter of
perspective.

When you spend 24 hours a day waiting, 144 hours a week, and
nearly 9,000 hours a year, with each hour at least 60 minutes long,

time drags. In our mechanistic society all hours are presumably the same length. But the humanist knows that some hours are short and that other hours stretch out interminably. Not all hours are the same. And so the men in Perote waited long hours for their release, waited and waited some more. Up in Texas the Republic's Congress appropriated release money for the prisoners, news which likely reached to Perote, but the money never arrived. News of their plight reached Washington, which tends to be more sympathetic than Austin to problems of the tempest-tossed. President John Tyler instructed Waddy Thompson, United States Minister to Mexico, to negotiate for release of the Texas prisoners, even though they were not his fellow citizens and he was not their representative. He was also to demand, not negotiate, release of any imprisoned citizens of the United States. As for home and Texas, the prisoners felt that President Sam Houston had abandoned them and was taking no steps toward their release. After all, the Texan Santa Fe Expedition and the Mier Expedition had not been Sam Houston's idea, and he did not approve of unofficial filibusters. Houston was not a Texan romantic.

From time to time the men plotted escape, one way of relieving tedium. The remarkable thing is that in their letters home they showed no reluctance to mention plans to break out. This provides the clearest indication that they did not expect the Mexicans to read their letters. The fact that a large proportion of Mexico's soldiery was illiterate would also bring a certain confidence that letters would not be read, particularly when they were written in a language not the Mexicans' own. Further, and this the men would not have considered, censorship would have been difficult even for bilingual Mexicans because the execrable spelling practiced by most Texans, who themselves would probably be called functional illiterates today, is difficult for educated Texans to decipher in the 1970's.

On July 2, 1843, sixteen Texans escaped through a hole bored in the wall; eight were recaptured. Eight months later another sixteen men escaped through a tunnel; seven were recaptured. This escape came two days after the Mexicans released a huge cache of Texas prisoners from Bexar, and could be ascribed to disappointment on the part of those remaining, except that you don't dig a tunnel in two days. In mid-September, 1844, the remaining Texas prisoners, about 105, started home with Mexico's blessing.

We lack good records that would enable us to state with precision how many died in prison—from disease, malnutrition, or exposure;

how many escaped; how many were released; and how many were killed by Mexican guards for any number of reasons. Naturally we do not know how many of those who did escape got lost or met the sharp blade of a machete or otherwise failed to reach home. In short, the list of MIA's from the Perote experience remains unreconciled.

Anyone seeking a sophisticated approach to racial antipathies should read neither the letters of the prisoners nor this book. These men had grievances, and they spilled over into racial charges. Since the Anglo-Texans suffered at the hands of Mexicans, they naturally didn't care for Mexicans. Few prisoners love their jailer. Besides that, regardless of the merits of either cause, you have a situation such as Richard A. Barkley's. His father and a brother were killed at the Alamo, and another brother fell with J. W. Fannin at Goliad. These misfortunes had happened only six years earlier, and again were due to Mexican action. Add to this past distress the fact that on March 22, 1843, Barkley writes home that he expects to be "liberated in about eleven days," and that on the following June 18, considerably more than eleven days later, he is still writing from the castle of Perote that "our treatment grows worse the longer [we] stay [.] the hours we have to work is increast to near double and iff one of us should be a little complaining he is forced of to work at the point of the bayonet and iff he proves to be two sick to work he is sent to the Hospitall where one of us that is well is not permitted to go even should he be like to dy. . . . On last Thursday we war locked up all day it being a day of feast–to-day we are locked up [.] this is the day they proclame the new constatution."

And then Barkley adds the eternal sentence, "Iff I am not mistaken this is the last leter I shall write at least I hope so." Only this time an ominous note follows: "None of the boys of our Prairie will go with me it being a haserdeous undertaking." Earlier Barkley had complained that he was made to "work nerlly every day and made to *pack* as mutch as we posablly can–to add to our mizery a large body of cavelry has binn stationed [.] We have there filth to carey out every morning."

Once earlier when Barkley had tried to escape, his fellow prisoners had "stopt" him. The result was, said Barkley, that the "Mexicans point me out and say I am the worst one in the Castle–I have worn hobels two weaks binn [beat] with there spades and muskets Calaboosed and ev[ery means to] cow me that they can think of–some of them–you need not to write to me any more for I think that I shall make my escape. There is no hopes of release." Small wonder then that he writes in another place, "I will have revenge or I will dy in the attempt."

Barkley sums up his feelings in a letter of April 10: "if you receive this letter remember it is from a friend in fine health and good spirits yet he is in Prison and in chanes and subject to insults of a people he hates worse than he possebly could [describe] a people that has murdered his only brother in cole blood [and] butchered his Father himself driven before the bayonets [many hundred] miles and that two without a blanket or a coat to sheald him from the weather fedd on the refused Flower that was full of Bugs and worms with a small quantity of beef."

As Barkley says, his captors order him about "with more authority than an over seer driving his negrowes." To the Mexicans he is an invader to be treated like a "conveck," but to himself, with that self-deception that we all practice, he "is as inicant as a child unborned."

So don't read the book which follows with any idea that it is going to be fair and dispassionate. Maybe these men imprisoned at the old fortress should not have been in Mexico, but nonetheless there they were for reasons that seemed sufficient for them. They had marched in chains, and had wound up in a region which one described as colder than Texas in the winter, a windswept area only 160 miles east-by-south from Mexico City, to be sealed off from their world by walls that were 12 feet high and 6 feet thick, with 96 cannon mounted on the periphery. The moat, approximately 100 feet wide and 20 feet deep, could be crossed only by a drawbridge leading in to the one large gate. At the entrance two huge statues had been carved, effigies in stone of two colonial soldiers who had been executed for sleeping while on guard. The Texans probably found little reassurance in that. Rumor holds that the Aztecs called the place *pinahuizapan*, or "something-to-be-buried-in."

As two Anglo observers wrote after a visit more than thirty years ago, "Today old Perote Prison is ignominious—its pits deserted— . . . The very atmosphere around it is unfit for human life; . . . and no living thing remains within its once-impregnable walls. Its moat is a dusty, rock-strewn ditch where a few mangy goats sometimes wander. The two huge sentinels in stone at the gate have become caricatures in rock."

But Perote would have one more flirtation with life. When Mexico declared war against the Axis powers, Perote prison was refurbished quickly but not too comfortably to house any Germans or Japanese soldiers who might fall into Mexican hands. Not many did.

To exist in Perote men had marched from the rather comfortable area of central Texas across the plains and mountains to Santa Fe and down through the desert of northern Mexico, at least 2,000 miles. You walk 2,000 miles under less than ideal conditions, and you wind up at Perote. This is not what most of them had in mind.

Or if they had joined the Mier Expedition, they had walked again from central Texas to the Rio Grande border, possibly 300 miles, to get captured in a fight in which they were outnumbered almost ten to one. They had watched their supplies run out and their discipline fall apart, and had surrendered to the forces of General Pedro Ampudia. Although they would later claim that they had surrendered as prisoners of war, they signed no terms of capitulation until after their arms had been grounded, when the Mexicans told them that they would be treated with "consideration." Back in Austin President Houston would take the position that the men had acted without authority, which really freed Mexico from obligation to treat them as prisoners of war.

General Ampudia sentenced all of the Mier prisoners to death, but as a sort of delayed Christmas present on December 27, 1842, reversed the execution decree. And then they marched. On the way a whole host of them escaped, but in trying to circle through the mountains during the dry season they became separated, lost their way, and suffered badly. In the end only three members made good their escape back to Texas. Altogether 176 Texans were recaptured, a rather discouraging figure.

Again they were sentenced to death, but then the execution order was modified to kill every tenth man, as chosen by lottery. One hundred seventy-six beans were placed in an earthen jar, seventeen of them black. A black bean meant death. Commissioned officers were ordered to draw first. As others drew, Big-Foot Wallace, astute as always, noticed that black beans were larger than white beans. Accordingly he fingered several beans before deciding successfully on the one to take out. Seventeen men were neither as shrewd nor as fortunate.

The Mexicans gave some of them time to write their families, and nearly all commissioned some companion to take a message back home if he ever returned there. The Mexicans then unshackled the doomed men from their companions, placed them in another courtyard, and at dusk on March 25, 1843, shot them. Five years later Mexico returned the bodies to Texas, and they are buried at Monument Hill near LaGrange, otherwise known as the home of the historic Chicken Ranch. Obviously not everyone loses at LaGrange.

But again, after this not altogether happy interlude, the Mier filibusters were marched on to the vicinity of Mexico City, where they did road work throughout the summer months before winding up at Perote in September 1843. To them Perote was not so much a shelter as an end of a long road.

The Dawson party has a somewhat different history. After General Adrian Woll invaded Texas in September 1842, capturing San Antonio, news reached LaGrange, where Nicholas Mosby Dawson gathered fifty-three men to head west to confront the enemy. A detachment of Mexican cavalry discovered his group when it was about a mile and a half from the fighting. Although the Texans took cover in a mesquite grove, the Mexicans withdrew from rifle range and with two pieces of artillery killed about half of the Texans. Dawson tried to surrender, but his men wouldn't cease firing. Naturally the Mexicans began firing again, continuing even after some of the Texans had dropped their arms. Thirty-five of the fifty-three were killed, and fifteen more were captured, five of them wounded. With this miserable beginning the prisoners were marched to Mexico to be held in Perote. Only nine ever made it home. From this standpoint, they too had marched a thousand miles to nowhere.

Among the prisoners who returned home from the Mier expedition was William Preston Stapp. In October 1844 he wrote his story. The next year his little book was published in type that would destroy the eyes of an ordinary person. The publisher was G. B. Zieber and Company in Philadelphia, and the printer was C. Sherman, 19 St. James Street, presumably in Philadelphia. Probably this book did not have wide circulation, for few copies have survived. In 1887–1888 the LaGrange *Journal* reprinted Stapp's story in its columns. In 1933 the *Journal* republished the book in a facsimile edition taken from its files. The price was $1.03 per copy, prepaid, and 75 cents per copy in orders of ten or more, postage prepaid.

The book paces well. It even has its poetic moments, and reads almost rhapsodically about the beauties of Mexico nights and Mexico City. But it is also relentless in its denunciation of Santa Anna and not much more charitable toward the expedition's captors. It presents a lively portrait of an unfortunate period in Texas-Mexican relations when both countries were shaking down and had not yet found their way. To understand some of the inherent tenseness that exists between Texas and Mexico, this book provides clues. While it won't please the Mexican nationalists on either side of the Rio Grande, perhaps it will make them slightly more tolerant of some of the extreme attitudes perpetuated even today by Texans who lack the courage to forget. And who knows, maybe the Mexican-baiters among today's Texans will perceive that historically those Mexicans stand on sound principle when they insist that Texans are arrogant and deceitful.

But see for yourself.

JOE B. FRANTZ
May, 1977

BOOK I

Chapter I

The Texan War of Independence, which opened with the battle of
Gonzales, October 1st, 1835, and closed with the rout of San Jacinto,
April 21st, 1836, was a drama too pregnant with decisive consequences to both belligerents to leave either in a mood or condition
for its immediate renewal. The army of invasion, with which Santa
Anna had entered the insurgent province, comprised not only the
choice troops, but nearly the whole disposable force of the Mexican
Republic. Every soldier of the regular line, not absolutely indispensable to the domestic guard service—every tenant of the prisons—
with the whole militia contingent his powers of conscription enabled him to levy—were embodied in the force which this infuriate
Attila brought to exterminate the gallant opponents of his usurpa-
tion and despotism. The spirit of those revolutionists he had quelled,
and over whose subjugated necks he had strode into the dictator's
chair, had rallied anew in the most formidable quarter of his dominions, and its dawning achievements menaced alike the integrity of
his empire, and the security of his power. The work of national
emancipation was begun afresh,—its sympathies lurked in the very
atmosphere of his capital, and all things sunk subordinate to its
prompt and effectual extinction. With characteristic vigour and sagacity he set out upon his bloody crusade, provided with all the imposing means within his reach, for the consummation of his designs.
The butcheries of Goliad and Bexar, the carnage and devastation that

marked his triumphal career from the San Antonio to the Jacinto, bear mournful witness of the magnitude of his preparations and the resistless numbers of his array. The tragic sequel of the short but sanguinary struggle, involving in one common ruin the invader and his cohorts, is too familiar to bear a recapitulation. An hour of dread retribution on the plains of San Jacinto placed the Mexican leader an unconditional captive in the hands of his enemies; and scarce a succeeding fortnight elapsed ere his last fugitive soldier had mounted the western bank of the Rio Grande.

However brilliant the renown which the valour, wisdom, and fortitude of this *six months'* campaign had flung over the arms of the young Anglo-American Republic, her condition at its close unequivocally demanded the adoption of a policy most likely to bring repose to her shattered energies, recruit her wasted strength, and enable her to secure, through an improved organization, those national advantages achieved by her unparalleled heroism. Brief as was the conflict, its intense and concentrated action—its rapid and frightful alternations of victory and defeat—its conflagrations of her towns —destruction of her citizen soldiery, and general paralysis of her industrial prosperity, left her a work of ruin to restore, that needed peace and her undistracted attention to facilitate.

Despite the nonfulfilment of most of the articles of the convention, entered into between President Santa Anna and the Texan Cabinet, (scrupulously fulfilled on the part of the latter, and faithlessly violated by the former in all the important pledges proposed by him,) other causes concurred to bestow upon Mexico and Texas, respectively, that respite from military operations, so acceptable to the people of both, and so highly and peculiarly advantageous to Texas. The costly and disastrous experiment essayed by Mexico, to stifle the freedom of the infant republic by one gigantic swoop of ravage and invasion, recoiled upon her with so retaliatory a shock of ruin and disgrace as left her equally unable as unwilling to try the hazard of a second venture. The immolated thousands of her conscripts, whose bones were left to bleach upon the plains her puissant resentment had devoted to the scourge of war—her captive battalions gorging every stronghold of Texas, appealed less eloquently to her fears and apprehensions than did the terror-stricken fugitives who returned from the foray, spreading their tales of consternation amongst their appalled countrymen, and magnifying the prowess and chivalry of their victorious foe, into deeds of invincibility, that froze the heart and blanched the cheek of their most dauntless auditors. Superior as was her power, and supercilious as were her hauteur and insolence, the blow they had received had humbled her too low for any immediate vindication. The popular excitements in her interior, with the embarrassed state of her foreign relations, likewise contributed their share to confine for a period of nearly six years the form of her hostility to Texas to empty proclamations and a few predatory demonstrations on the frontier.

Texas was no sooner cleared of the grim realities of war, than she applied herself with an activity and intelligence unsurpassed, to the organization of her government, the recognition by foreign powers of her independence; and the earnest achievement of all the blessings of peace and freedom, for which she had so heroically encountered the vengeance and injuries of her powerful foe. The story of her romantic devotion to liberty; the promptness with which she entered upon her seemingly hopeless resistance to oppression; her unshrinking courage and unyielding firmness through the most imminent perils and overwhelming disasters; her romantic generosity in the intoxication of victory, and the glory and lustre of her unaided emancipation from the thraldom of the tyrant, had collectively so dignified and adorned her struggle in the eyes of the world, as to excite an intense and universal solicitude for her welfare. Scarcely had the wisdom of her civil councils perfected the symmetry and order of her institutions, ere the door of the halls of nations was flung open for her admission; and her youthful hands clasped in the glaived embrace of the most august and powerful governments of the earth. Population poured its impetuous and fertilizing streams upon her shores; towns and cities sprung like magic from her surface, her plains and valleys teemed with the choicest treasures of agriculture, and all the bounteous arts of life that an expanding enterprise, commerce, and navigation can supply, began augmenting her resources, and expanding her prosperity. To a climate and soil whose salubrity and fertility suffers from any attempt at embellishment, with prairies and uplands, streams, hills, and skies, whose gorgeous beauty wrung frequent exclamations of delight and amazement from the wretched Santa Anna himself, Texas unites a government matchless for the wisdom and liberality of its provisions, reciprocally blessing and sustained by a people, the most chivalrous and generous amongst the families of men. What marvel then if her strides in advancement, not only uneclipsed, but unexampled in the history of nations, should overawe for a time an unrelenting but enervate adversary, whose polluting step she had chastised from her realm, in the very *childhood* of her existence.

Though his guardian angel of revolution not long after his return, again lifted Santa Anna into supreme authority at home, and his dastardly menaces were from time to time fulminated against the tranquillity and sovereignty of Texas, she continued unchecked in her career of aggrandizement, mocking at his threats, and defying his idle bravadoes. With her small but gallant navy, she chased his shipping from the seas, blockaded his harbours, and insulted his pusillanimous flag, by every provoking taunt and challenge she could contrive. Since his own departing footprints were graven upon the beach of Velasco, six years of uninterrupted peace and fulness had rolled over Texas; ere from the Gulf to the mountains, or from the Sabine to the Bravo, the recurring sun's broad eye had looked upon the form of a hostile Mexican.

As incompetent to emancipate his malignant soul from the memory of his ignominious defeat and capture, as he is incapable of the moral effort of gratitude or faith; too cowardly to avenge his misfortunes, and too ignoble to forgive them, Santa Anna throughout this period garrisoned the Mexican towns along the Rio Grande, with large bodies of vagabond and degenerate mercenaries; instructed to cross, plunder, and harass the Texan frontier, at whatever defenceless points his *rabble canaille* could effect a descent with impunity. This vanguard of his vapouring Excellency's oft-announced re-invasion, so seldom extended their incursions beyond the Nueces, and so precipitately retraced their steps on the slightest intimation of their skulking presence being known, that the people of the frontier most accessible to their assaults, not only regarded their vicinity without apprehension, but came in time to disband every form of military police, which previous precaution had instituted for the protection of their property, so free from all alarm or anxiety was the public mind, in regard to these formidable bands, recruited and posted for the ostensible object of redeeming the lost honour of Mexico, but hitherto signalizing their chivalry by no more valiant exploits than an occasional act of rapine, undertaken with the profoundest secrecy, conducted with consummate caution, and promptly abandoned on the first approach of discovery or resistance.

The spring of 1842 opened with considerable reinforcements to these garrisons, followed by a more imposing proclamation of invasion than usual; and by authentic information received from various parts in the interior of Mexico, of preparations actually making by the Dictator, for putting into execution his long-meditated assault. So grave an aspect had these demonstrations excited, that a proclamation was issued by the Executive of Texas, detailing the apprehended danger, and inviting the people in the various military districts to organize for defence; and more particularly advising the raising a volunteer force to protect the western frontier, until the country could be placed in an efficient condition for the reception of the enemy. In compliance with his recommendation, several small detachments of volunteers were dispatched to the frontier, to act as corps of observation, and afford such protection to the border, as their limited numbers could give.

Previous to their march, and very early in the spring, General Bascus, the Mexican officer in command at Presidio Rio Grande, (a northern post upon the river of that name,) crossed the Rio Grande at the head of a large body of troops, variously exaggerated by rumour, and penetrating by forced marches the wilderness lying between Presidio and Bexar, succeeded in surprising that defenceless town, dispersing its population, and pillaging and carrying off whatever property their rapid retreat allowed them to transport. This predatory attack, trifling as it was in its result, excited no inconsiderable alarm in the minds of the people residing on the San Antonio, and by its audacity and the force employed in its execution, generally contributed to strengthen the existing apprehensions of a general invasion. Being followed up, however, by no second demonstration from the quarter from which it proceeded, public anxiety became concentrated on the lower route, between Mier and Matamoras, where General Canales was reported to be in force, and waiting for the subsiding of the waters, swollen by the heavy spring rains, to advance into Texas. In the mean while a volunteer corps under the command of General Davis, had taken up a position on the west bank of the Nueces, near San Patricio, watching the motions of Canales, through their spies on the Rio Grande, and communicating them to the government. These men, amounting to something less than two hundred, wholly unsupported, destitute of artillery, and encamped in the open prairie near the river, unprotected by any form of works, elicited the attention of Canales, who regarding them as an easy prey, advanced to their capture or destruction, near the 8th of the month of July. The Texans, advised of his approach, abandoned their camp at the close of day, leaving their tents standing, and camp-fires burning, and retiring to a more secure station under the second bluff of the river, lay upon their arms during the night, ready to avail themselves of whatever advantages a night attack from the enemy might afford them. Though in the immediate vicinity of their camp with a force of near a thousand men, of cavalry and infantry, Canales, distrusting the deceitful quiet of their noiseless tents, and apprehensive of an ambuscade, permitted the night to wear off without any attempt to molest them. Early on the following morning, as a party of the Texans were bringing off some provisions and cooking-utensils from the tents, a combined assault was made upon them by the whole Mexican force, aided by the fire of several pieces of artillery, so disposed as to rake the encampment. The party in quest of provisions reached their comrades in safety, disclosing his mistake to the Mexican leader; who immediately reversing his order of battle, bore down upon Davis and his men with equal fury he had just bestowed upon the empty camp. The Texans received him with characteristic coolness and reserve, waiting until his lines approached within fifty or sixty yards, when a volley from their unerring rifles emptied a score or two of saddles, and drove the broken infantry some distance to the rear of their artillery. Here they remained formed out of reach of rifle-shot, directing their harmless cannon against the Texans, who advancing in platoons after each discharge of their guns, shot down the men who served them, and regained their cover, before a second discharge could be brought to bear on them. The engagement lasted in this form for something above an hour; when the Mexicans began a disorderly retreat, covered by their cavalry, whose superior numbers checked any attempt at pursuit.

This discomfiture of General Canales terminated all further attempt against the tranquility of the frontier during the summer; and quiet and confidence were again restored to the border settlements. But the irrepressible enterprise of the Mexican brigands, revived with the recall and disbandment of the Texan pickets, who had hitherto so effectually restrained them. Early in September, General Adrian Woll, with a band of some 1,300 men, (a part of General Bascus's force,) pursuing the same route taken by that Parthian robber in the preceding spring, surprised Bexar again, and after a sharp conflict with the citizens, compelled them to capitulate to his overwhelming numbers. The District Court being in session at the time, had collected in the town a number of persons drawn there by business, who after uniting with the population in a short but manly resistance, became necessarily fellow-victims to the surrender.

Relying on the time that must elapse before any adequate force could be raised in the interior and despatched to chastise his temerity, Woll encamped at Bexar, for the purpose of extending his pillage over a broader theatre than his more timid predecessor had accomplished. Near a week was thus passed in refreshing and loading his banditti, when advices reached him that Colonel Caldwell, with a hundred and four volunteers hastily raised near Gonzales, had reached the neighbourhood of Bexar, and taken up a position on the Salado, a small creek in the vicinity, to await reinforcements preparatory to attacking him. The Mexican deeming this a rare opportunity for mingling some laurels with his plunder, left the town with a competent guard, and marching directly for the camp of Caldwell, was enabled by his superiority of force entirely to surround it. Here a desultory combat raged between this handful of riflemen and twelve hundred of their assailants for near three days. A company of fifty-three Texans, under the command of Captain Dawson, from La Grange, in attempting to cut their way to Caldwell, were enclosed in a regiment of Mexicans six hundred strong; when, with the aid of a field-piece, they were literally hewed to pieces; battling with Spartan courage to the last, and leaving but fourteen survivors, twelve badly wounded, as prisoners, and two who effected their escape from the field. With near four hundred of his men left dead on the banks of the Salado, Woll began his retreat on the third day; pursued to the very suburbs of Bexar, by the intrepid Texans. Here the disconcerted Mexicans paused no longer than was required to secure their prisoners and baggage, when they abandoned the town and prosecuted their retreat as rapidly as the incumbrances to their march admitted of. Colonel Caldwell entered the village as soon as it was evacuated, and being joined during the same night by an accession of force, recommenced the pursuit on the following day. Having come up with Woll on the Rio Hondo, some sixty miles from Bexar, he found the Mexicans too strongly entrenched in a swamp, to afford any hope of dislodging them with his feeble command; and having called a council of his officers, it was decided to relinquish for the present, any further retaliation upon the retreating freebooters.

This incursion of Woll, though involving the most trifling loss of

life on the part of the Texans, as contrasted with that suffered by the invaders, roused an exasperated spirit throughout the country, that called for immediate measures of redress. With no regular force with which to garrison these frontier towns–with a scattered and scanty population, liable at all periods to the attack of these insolent and lawless marauders, it was obvious to all that security of person and property was not otherwise to be obtained than by carrying the war into the enemy's country, and inflicting upon his own citizens some memorable chastisement. Amongst the fifty-two prisoners carried off into captivity by Woll, not only were all the leading and influential citizens of Bexar, but as we before intimated, the entire District Court, then and there in session, judges, lawyers, clerks, sheriffs, and all. Torn from their homes and families with the perspective of a Mexican dungeon before them, the inevitable rigour of their unmerited lot, contributed with the lamentations of their agonized friends, to quicken into a flame the indignation which previous annoyances had engendered. An act of the most govelling barbarity on the part of the Mexican commander at Bexar aided to hasten this rising storm of retribution. Residing in the town at the time of its capture was an old and most respectable citizen, a Mexican by birth, an adherent to the Federal Constitution of 1824, and necessarily a foe to the usurper of his country's liberties, and an exile from his despotism. Though a Texan citizen by sympathy, loyalty, and residence, throughout her struggle with Mexico, he had borne arms with neither, preserving his neutrality with the strictest fidelity, and most unswerving honour. His only child, a daughter of some sixteen summers, the beautiful, accomplished, and peerless belle of that western wild, the pride and solace of his declining life; as tenderly devoted to the gallant author of her being, as she was ardently cherished in return, participated in her father's captivity to the Mexican chief. The daughter's fatal attractions led to a betrayal of the father's birth and political history. The latter was promptly placed in the strictest confinement, whilst his liberation and life were pressed by the enamoured ruffian upon the anguished girl, as the reward of her acquiescence in his wishes. They were left behind when the monster was chased from Bexar, to curse in heartbroken ruin their remorseless captor.

In obedience to the general expression of public sentiment, President Houston issued a proclamation inviting volunteers for a retaliatory expedition across the Rio Grande, and designating the 25th of

Chapter I

October, at San Antonio de Bexar, as the time and place for their rendezvous. Near eight hundred of the most gallant spirits of western Texas responded to the requisition, with whom the author found himself associated in an enterprise which, however disastrously it afterwards terminated, wore at its outset the most attractive hues of daring chivalry and high adventure.

Chapter II

San Antonio de Bexar, the place of our rendezvous, (so memorable as the scene of numerous sanguinary conflicts,) is a town of great antiquity, extending on either side of the river San Antonio, some ten miles above the mouth of the Medina, and upwards of a hundred from the sea-coast. Early in the present century its population is reported to have been large, but the harassing disturbances to which it has been subjected have gradually reduced its numbers, until the present census scarcely reaches fifteen hundred. The houses are generally of stone, strong, capacious, and built in the old Spanish style, square or oblong, one story high, and with terraced roofs. The two segments of the town, separated by the river, (some sixty yards wide here,) are again united by a wooden bridge; and grim midst the scattered suburbs on the eastern bank, still frown the blackened ruins of the historic fortress of the Alamo. From here, in the opening of October, 1835, the vaunting Cos, at the head of his horde of mercenaries, announced his design of making Texas a wilderness, and sweeping from her soil the last vestige of population; and scarce two months rolled away ere he and his captive comrades deployed through its gates, naked of all but their dishonoured lives, bestowed by the clemency of their victors. Here, a few months later, the heroic Travis and his gallant band of patriot spirits beat back the Mexican dictator with his swarming thousands, until, literally spent with carnage, they piled their immortal forms upon one gory hecatomb, and sunk to sleep in everlasting fame. The glorious reminiscences connected with this fortress, so honourable to Texan, and so disgraceful to Mexican valour, provoked the barbarian Filisola, on his retreat from Texas after the field of San Jacinto, to order its walls to be prostrated, and its brass artillery train destroyed, and this too in wanton infraction of the armistice then pending between the countries. Vain hope to strip the old pile of its lustrous renown; since, though not a solitary monumental stone were left standing to betray its site of fame, amongst the imperishable plates of history will it endure, chronicled and illustrated to the latest time.

Hoary with age, defaced by war, and partially dilapidated, rise from out of the muskeet groves round Bexar the gray and massive forms of those military churches, the Missions. Reared long since in the depths of the wilderness by the courageous monks of the order of Jesus, they served alternately for the holy ministrations of knowledge and religion, and as impregnable asylums against the sudden fury or wily treachery of their swarthy congregations. Many a vanished year has come and gone since monk and red man fled together from their thresholds, and left their desecrated shrines and broken portals open to all whose choice or necessity might urge to enter. Gone are their old green woods, beneath whose starlit glades the Indian maiden and her Spanish swain were wont to meet. The tall wild grass shoots rankly above the mouldering mounds where sleep the silent shepherds of vanquished flocks. And voiceless, save with the hoot of the melancholy owl, are those ragged belfries, where pealed of yore sweet chimes of bells, to call the lagging herdsman and hunter to their prayers. They are four in number, Conception, San Jose, San Juan, and Espada, all situated to the south of the town, and straggling some three miles apart, along the banks of the San Antonio. Near the first mentioned, the most contiguous to the village, was achieved the brilliant and decisive victory by Fanning and Bowie over General Cos and a large body of his forces, a short time anterior to the storming of Bexar and its surrender to the Texans.

San Antonio de Bexar is the extreme northwestern town of Texas. Between the river on which it stands and the Rio Grande stretches a wilderness, whose mean breadth is computed at a hundred and fifty miles. Rolling prairies of rich sandy loam, clothed with luxuriant grass, and intersected by clear and rapid streams, whose banks abound with timber, make up the general features of this uninhabit-

ed district. Along its western boundary rolls the majestic and solitary Bravo, upon whose banks were situated the rich and populous
Mexican villages against which our expedition was destined to oper-
ate.

The command of this foray having been entrusted by the President, to Brigadier-General Alexander Somerville, (then deemed an
officer of courage and ability,) and all the volunteers being arrived
at Bexar by the 11th of November, an election of regimental officers
was held, which resulted as follows: James R. Cook, of Washington,
was chosen Colonel; George T. Howard, of Bexar, Lieutenant-Colo-
nel, and D. L. Murphree, of Victoria, Major. The regiment of drafted
men who made up the other division of the corps, was commanded
by Colonel Bennett, (of Montgomery county), and the aggregate
force when mustered, reached to a fraction above eight hundred
men. This little army, so officered, and every man mounted and
equipped with rifle, knife, and pistols, with a hundred rounds of ammunition each, moved from the San Antonio on the 13th of November, 1842.

Our march, but for that cheeriness which an advance never fails
to inspire in the bosom of a soldier, was monotonous, and unexcit-
ing in the extreme. Not a single instrument of military music accompanied the troops, neither trumpet, fife, nor drum, to wake the
echoes of the morn with the inspiring reveille, or salute the drowsy
ear at close of day with the animating strains of the tattoo. Even
the stimulating presence of danger was lacking; our spies scouring
the pathless waste far and near, without reporting the dimmest trail
of a foe. The 4th of December brought us to the Nueces, over which
a very tolerable bridge had been constructed, by the advance companies of Captains Mitchell and Robertson; and having crossed,
men, baggage, and horses, we devoted the interval of a day to recruiting our wearied limbs, and regaling the cavalry, on the luxuriant
pasturage furnished by its shores.

Some five days before reaching the Nueces, our route, which had
previously lain over an elevated rolling table-land, studded at intervals with beautiful clumps of live-oak, post oak, and muskeet, was
suddenly intercepted by one of those unseemly bogs, whose frequency through this wilderness during the rainy season, is of itself
as efficient a barrier to the passage of troops unfamiliar with the
country, as would be most of the defences concerted by man.

Crossing a creek near Navarro's old ranch, on the morning of the

27th of November, after a previous day of unintermitted rain, we struck into a poor and sandy prairie, where, before proceeding a mile, we became fairly engulfed in one of those deceitful quagmires. Stretching out to an indefinite distance on every side of us, going forward was quite as safe as turning back; and sinking through the grass at every step, the dismounted men above their knees, and our horses still deeper, we toiled and struggled onward. All order of progress was promptly abandoned; every man trusting to his own sagacity for his extrication, and devoting his undivided energies to his personal welfare. The line stretching above a mile in length, and coiling into the most fantastic curves; men, mules, and horses, half submerged, and all floundering as though possessed by a general nightmare, produced a spectacle of the most ludicrous aspect imaginable. It was not until near the close of a cold and drizzling day allotted us for this queer navigation, that we effected a landing. Many of our pack-mules stuck fast in the bog, and finding it impracticable to leave them, they were promptly shot, to preserve them against the slow and lingering deaths that awaited them. The congratulations after a brilliant victory could scarcely have exceeded those that followed our arrival upon terra firma; and though the rain fell in torrents throughout the night that followed, toils and the past were quickly forgotten, in a hearty supper and as hearty a sleep.

The morning after a day of repose upon the Nueces, Colonel Flacco, a Lipan chief, who, with several followers, had joined the expedition in the capacity of guides, arrived in camp with despatches from Captain Hays, (who commanded one of our spy companies,) and reported the capture of two Mexican rancheros, or herdsmen, whom they had taken in the neighbourhood of Loredo, a Mexican village some sixty miles from our position.

These rancheros stated the garrison of Loredo to be about eighty in number; neither they nor the inhabitants having the slightest intelligence or apprehension of our approach. A forced march for the village was instantly made, where we arrived within twelve miles on the evening of the 7th of December. Early on the following morning, we entered the town, which was surrendered without the discharge of a gun. One of our prisoners having effected his escape the previous night, had announced our advance; forewarned, the troops secured their retreat, carrying off a large supply of goods and provisions, with which the place was stored. Their horses had likewise been driven off during the night, save a few found concealed in the

houses, and yokes of oxen hid away in the capperel (a thicket) adjoining the town. This proved an irritating loss to our men, as many
of them were dismounted, their horses having given out on the way,
and the wearied riders being compelled to long marches, packing
their baggage and provisions on their shoulders. Many of them la-
boured under the additional inconvenience of having lost their
blankets and clothes; and as the winter had set in with unusual
severity, the absence of such indispensable comforts was keenly
felt. Added to this, our last day's provision was expended, and notwithstanding the voluntary bankruptcy of the town, the General
found it necessary to lay a requisition on its authorities for supplies.
Limited as was the demand, it was complied with reluctantly, and
in as stinted quantities as their fears allowed them to bring in. Having received it, we dropped down some three miles below, and encamped for the night.

On this march, a man of Captain Cameron's company, (De Boyce
by name,) was shot by the accidental discharge of a comrade's gun;
the ball passing near his heart, and killing him almost instantly. He
was the first member of the expedition who had fallen, and being
brought into camp, received a soldier's burial, with all accompanying honours and solemnities. Alas! poor fellow, these tributes of
respect were rendered him by some, whose bloody graves are yet un-
honoured, unsung, and unavenged.

The succeeding day our camp was the theatre of a scene, which,
but for its intimate connexion with the disasters that followed, I
would most cheerfully forbear to allude to.

The requisition upon the town having comprehended nothing beyond a very inadequate supply of provisions, those of the soldiery
most destitute of clothing, blankets, and other necessary supplies,
obtained leave in the morning to revisit Loredo, with no declared
object beyond that of examining the place. Upon their return to
camp, however, they came loaded with as various and motley an as-
sortment of pillage, as was ever brought within the lines of a civilized force. Blankets, beds, and bed-clothes, cooking utensils of various design; horses, mules, and asses; beeves, veals, and muttons;
poultry of every genus of ornithology; honey, bread, flour, sugar, and
coffee; saddles and bridles; coats, hats, and every other specimen
of male apparel known amongst the Mexicans; with miscellaneous
decorations in use amongst the gentler sex, that our blushing muse
forbids us to catalogue.

This body of toll-takers, to the number of near two hundred, riding into camp, driving the live-stock before them, and with their bodies enwrapped to treble the ordinary dimensions of men, their persons hung about with all the variegated drapery of Jew clothes-pedlars, and horses panting under pyramidal burdens, as queerly assorted as a Carolina *moover*, looked more like a troop of equestrian harlequins, than brave and manly soldiers, who had crossed desert, bog, and river, to chastise the insolence of their country's foes, and avenge the manes of their butchered brethren.

Nothing could exceed the mingled emotions of pity, diversion, and indignation, that filled the bosoms of those in camp, when this strange cavalcade of masquers reined up. The rude hand of unbridled license, the pitiless struggle of the strong arm with the weak, the *Vae victis* of war's worst excess, breathed eloquently from every feature of the dramatis personæ.

Some protested their merchandise was fairly paid for, and others found language too weak to applaud the munificence of the generous donors of their collections; but by far the greater number openly plead their necessities, and vindicated the pillage, as a fair retaliation for similar excesses suffered from the enemy. To the credit of many who participated in the outrage, be it said, that with a little reflection, they heartily united in condemning it, and voluntarily restored every article they had taken. The captains of companies received an immediate order to have all the property so seized, collected and brought to the guard-fire; where it was scrupulously returned to the citizens. Such portions only being detained as were required by the necessitous, and would have been embraced in the requisition of the preceding day, but for the alleged poverty of the dissembling foe.

After making restitution of the plundered property, our camp on the river was struck, and the army put in motion in an eastwardly direction. Murmurs and discontent were openly and loudly expressed at this retrograde movement; and General Somerville indignantly charged with the pusillanimous intent of an ignominious return home, without pulling a trigger on the enemy, or doing any thing that would subserve the objects, or reflect credit upon the expedition. His capacity for command, and his courage and conduct in the affair on hand, were freely criticised, and contemptuously denounced by men and officers, almost within his hearing. Venting their displeasure in mutinous threats and imprecations, the march was continued, through seemingly impenetrable thickets until 8 o'clock, P.M., when we halted for the night in the capperel, without forage for our horses, or water for ourselves. Here was another pretext for complaint, which furnished the most fruitful abuse of general and officers; which can only be truly appreciated by those who are familiar with the unbridled tongues of a volunteer camp. As soon as morning dawned, a search for water was ordered, and being readily found, our camp was moved to the pool, and all things postponed over a smoking breakfast. The mettle of men and officers was destined to show itself.

Breakfast being discussed, and a parade ordered, General Somerville proceeded in a short and animated address, to establish a proper understanding between himself and malcontents. He deprecated with seeming candour and apparent mortification, the futile and inglorious results which had thus far characterized our efforts. Appealed to his patriotism and soldierly honour, in proof of his eagerness to come up with the enemy, and concluded by declaring his desire to descend the river in quest of adventure, that might close the campaign with benefit to the country, and glory to themselves. When he had finished, all who felt desirous of prosecuting the war, and penetrating into the Mexican territory, were requested to retire upon a neighbouring hill. Near five hundred volunteers, responded to this call. It was next announced, that such as were anxious to return home, were at liberty to go; and this unwarlike privilege was immediately asserted by one hundred and fifty of the drafted men, under Colonel Bennett. A body of these drafted militia had abandoned the expedition at Bexar, even before it set out; and most of those who had accompanied it to the Rio Grande, insisted upon their orders extending no farther, and claimed their duty to be technically discharged by the capture and pillage of Loredo. Penetrating to this barrier, was an achievement never before performed by a Texan force; and the renown of the exploit (however ridiculous in other eyes), seemed to fill the measure of their most expanded dreams of glory.

A council of the officers of the volunteer force being held, it was resolved to descend the Bravo, capture Revilla, (or Guerero, as it is called,) and continue the descent to Mier and Camargo, unless intercepted and repulsed by a superior force. These towns, from Presidio to Matamoras, are distant from forty to sixty miles apart, and all, except Loredo, (which is within the Texan territory, though inhabited by Mexicans,) on the western bank of the Rio Grande. Their population is variously estimated at from twelve to eighteen hundred souls. The Mexicans, we felt assured, were by this time aware of our presence in their vicinity, and would not fail to bring up a competent force for their defence from the crowded garrisons below. To encounter their soldiery, and by one decisive engagement chastise them into peace, was the predominating desire of every heart, and, as well as could be ascertained, the fixed resolve of men and officers.

Our whole force moved down the left bank of the Bravo, bearing to the east of the settlements on the river, to obscure as much as possible our advance and point of destination from the enemy's spies. Colonel Bennett's command continued with us several days, and hopes were cherished that the contagious ardour of the volunteers might yet arrest their departure, and secure their important co-operation in the brilliant enterprise ahead. In this, however, we paid their chivalry an unmerited compliment, as on the morning of the 11th, those *fireside* patriots turned their faces home and their backs to the foe.

A bright December morning and a truant humour allured some comrades and myself to diverge from our line of march, and try our skill in woodcraft. Beside the droves of mustangs and wild cattle that still roam in freedom over these desert plains, deer, elk, turkeys, and Mexican hogs, are found in abundance wherever the hunter's enterprise may institute a search. These last abound in various parts of Texas, and are found in all the middle and northeastern states of Mexico. They seem to be a distinct genus of the porcine species, bearing as little resemblance to their kindred of the sty, in size or flavour, as they do in habit. Though seldom above a roasting pig in bulk, they defend themselves with the utmost courage when assailed, and if forced to fly exhibit extraordinary speed and activity. Their colour is uniformly a dirty gray, and their flesh so coarse and rancid as to revolt any appetite but one whetted by the extremest hunger. The panther is represented to hunt them with tireless industry, preferring their carcass above all other prey to be found in the forest.

A few hours' work sufficed to supply our utmost need, and building a fire at noon under the leafless crown of an old oak, we dined daintily upon a juicy deer-haunch, and rejoined our comrades loaded with turkeys and venison.

Continuing our march south for three days through bogs and

thickets of muskeet, we turned suddenly to the west, and struck the Bravo some six miles above Guerero, opposite an Indian village.

This noble river, which strongly resembles the Missouri in the complexion of its waters, and the arrowy swiftness of its current, though scarcely half its usual volume when we approached it, measured above three hundred yards across. Its source extends beyond the forty-second degree of northern latitude, and, receiving fewer tributaries in its course than any river on the American continent, it yet presents above its mouth a more open and uninterrupted channel than most of its class now used by navigators.

With three small boats procured at points below, our little force, reduced to five hundred men, proceeded to embark by companies, in the order maintained on the march. Captain McCullough, who had been despatched with ten men to reconnoitre Guerero, having lost his way through the ignorance of his guide, came up with us whilst crossing here.

By three o'clock P.M. two hundred of our men had reached the opposite bank, and were scarcely landed, before General Green and Captain Bogart, who had gone in the direction of the town with a small force, came hurrying in, pursued by the Mexican general Canales, with upwards of two hundred cavalry. Colonel Cook immediately formed our troops who had landed in order of battle, and calmly awaited the approach of the Mexicans. But the enemy, suddenly relinquishing their pursuit, halted at a distance of half a mile, and carefully noting our preparation, galloped off precipitately, nor were again heard of in that neighbourhood. The next morning, the remainder of the troops, with the rearguard and baggage, being crossed to the Mexican side, we all took up the line of march towards the town.

At a short distance from the village we were met by the alcalde, a Frenchman by birth, who formally surrendered the place, promising a full compliance with our requisition for provisions and stores, and earnestly entreating the commander would spare his fellow-citizens the terror of a visit from his men. His considerate prayer was granted, and we proceeded to pitch our camp on the Salado, a small stream about a mile below the town.

Chapter III

*Guerero · Presents to Officers · The
Requisition · Discontents of the men ·
Return home of General Somerville and
Companions · Election of Colonel Fisher to the
command · March upon Mier · Successful
stratagem of Ampudia · Battle of Mier ·
Surrender of the Texans.*

Guerero is some four miles from the Rio Grande, built upon the
southern bank of the Salado, a small and rapid stream, emptying
into the Bravo, at a southeasterly point between seven and ten miles
from the town. Its commerce, like most of the villages above Matamoras, is chiefly supported by the country along the river, which is
of surpassing fertility, and in many places judiciously and industri-
ously cultivated. Wheat, corn, oats, beans, potatoes, beef, and hides
form the staple commodities of trade, and must, at no distant day,
from their cheap and abundant production, make the valley of the
Rio Grande the most wealthy and prosperous portion of the Mexican Republic.

The night of our encampment upon the Salado, a number of the
officers visited Guerero, and returned loaded with presents of various kinds, amongst which were several of the finest mules we had
met with, elegantly and richly caparisoned. These were the concilia-
tory offerings of the town authorities, pressed upon their visiters
with an urgency that brooked no denial, and meant no doubt by the
terrified donors to avert from themselves the unhappy sack, to
which Loredo was subjected. The morning fully explained this munificence to our officers, in the sorry character of the requisition
brought into camp. Never was such an inventory of rubbish heaped
together as the peace offerings sent by the citizens of Guerero to
ransom their village from an inquisitorial visit. Some few dozen
tattered saddle-blankets, the same number of worn-out saddles, a

meagre supply of hats and shoes, with about two days' provisions, (all of which, lumped together, would scarce have repaid the trouble of burning them,) made up the compromise proposed by these help-less and fear-stricken creatures, in mitigation of the very moderate damages assessed against them. After their distribution had been made, and followed up by an order to fall back to the Rio Grande, the indignation of our men could scarce be repressed. Surely, argued they, if the interpretation the Mexicans themselves had practically asserted in Texas (for a victorious enemy over a vanquished one), were to be carried out, not a pound of provisions, a cent of treasure, or an ell of goods to be found within the range of our conquest, but were *legitimate spoils*. Suffering not only for the common comforts of a camp, but absolutely for indispensable articles of clothing, against the inclemency of the season, (all which the conquered town was fully able to spare us from its superfluous stores,) the men yet consented to retire. General Somerville, however, apprehensive of a reaction of sentiment, was not content until he had put the river be-tween his command and the place. Here we encamped amidst such universal confusion and discontent that it was late and with diffi-culty discipline was sufficiently restored to parade a guard. The rain fell in torrents, and a bleak northwesterly wind, piercing every cover we could erect, froze the very blood within our veins. Captain Hays' and Bogart's companies, who had recrossed the river and marched to town to receive the moneyed part of the requisition (five thousand dollars), returned as empty-handed as they went; the authorities of-fering them one hundred and seventy-three dollars, representing it as all the town contained. This was of course contemptuously re-fused.

Upon the arrival of these companies, and the guard which had been sent over to support them, a general order was issued for im-mediate preparations to return home. A rumour had reached Somer-ville that Ampudia was advancing from below, at the head of a large force, and whether apprehensive of being overpowered, or disgusted with the disorganization and disaffection that prevailed around him, our commander, with above a hundred followers, determined to re-linquish all further operations on the Mexican frontier, and retrace his steps to Texas. Except with a limited number of his personal friends and adherents, the General had become odious to men and officers; and most of those who resolved to accompany him back, cordially sympathized in the contempt and distrust so universally meted out to him. With his staff and the associates in his fears or longings, he set out upon the 19th of December, and, after being several times deposed on the way by his mutinous followers, and Colonel Flacco (the Lipan chief,) substituted in his stead, reached Bexar and disbanded his force, pursued into retirement by the scorn of the very men who participated in his desertion.

The remainder of the volunteers, amounting to three hundred, were all resolved upon prosecuting their march down the river, and endeavouring to accomplish something, that would redeem the expedition from the contempt which all felt must otherwise stigmatize its history. Accordingly, on the morning of the 20th, the six companies of Cameron, Eastland, Reece, Pierson, Ryon, and Buster, proceeded to elect a commander, and Colonel Fisher was unanimously chosen for the office, a highly accomplished gentleman and most gallant soldier. Fisher had served his country both in the cabinet and field, with a courage and efficiency, second to that of no man who partook of its revolutionary trials. In the charge at San Jacinto, he was first in the Mexican camp; and throughout all the distracting blunders of the present expedition, foremost with his counsel and example in conciliating the disaffected, animating the despondent, and daring every fatigue, toil, and danger, to secure success and triumph to our arms. Possessing the unbounded respect of officers and men, and regarded with the highest adoration for his honour, humanity, and enterprise, his election inspired our little troop with a confidence and intrepidity that flung over the future the happiest auguries.

By the 22d, we were on our march to Mier. General Green, with a small force, dropped down the river in the boats, whilst the main body followed in the rear on the east bank of the river, to collect horses and such provisions from the *ranches* as we stood in need of. In passing a small settlement of Carancawa Indians (the largest and finest-looking savages in either Mexico or Texas) one of our men got possession of the memorable British flag, which afterwards came so near rupturing the good understanding between the English ambassador and the Mexican court. It was a faded and tattered ensign, and little dreamed of by any through whose hands it passed, as likely to engender contention of any kind.

The morning of the 23d found us on the Mexican bank of the Rio Grande, seven miles above Mier, where, leaving our camp equipage and horses under a small guard, we moved down upon the town, and by ten o'clock had occupied it without resistance. The entire absence of any thing resembling a panic, with the quiet and unembarrassed air of the citizens who greeted our *entrée* into their village, was so unusual and unexpected, as to inspire a distrust in the minds of many of the source of their tranquillity.

Though our scouts had been unable to detect the presence of a foe, we implicitly relied upon finding the place garrisoned; and notwithstanding our disappointment, felt sure of his *vicinity*, and that too, in no inconsiderable numbers.

Colonel Canales had passed through the town a few days previous with a force superior to our own; and Ampudia was known to be in the neighbourhood with one *ten times* as great. Under such circumstances, General Fisher called up the alcalde, and presenting him a requisition for a few horses and a supply of provisions, (which were unhesitatingly promised,) evacuated the town, and re-crossing the Rio Grande, pitched his camp due east from Mier about four miles. As a precautionary measure, the alcalde was carried with us to camp, and detained as a hostage for the delivery of the provisions, as stipulated, on the following day. On the 24th instant, a party of our spies on the Mexican bank were surprised by the enemy, and two of them (Holderman and Lewis) captured; whilst the rest narrowly effected their escape. This was the first certain intelligence we had of the presence of the foe. Captain Baker's spy company, on the same day, discovered a trail passing in the direction of our previous camp, (seven miles above Mier,) which we afterwards learned was made by Ampudia's force, who, ignorant of our removal, had gone up to attack us, or by a display of superior numbers, induce us to abandon the neighbourhood. The morning of the 25th, we commenced our march towards the point agreed upon for the delivery of the requisition. This was at the mouth of the Alcantro, a small stream emptying into the Rio Grande a short distance below our camp, and upon whose southern bank, some three miles from its confluence, the town of Mier is situated. We had advanced but a little way, before our videttes captured a Mexican, who reported Ampudia in Mier, with a force of a *few hundred* men, with whom he was determined to maintain the town, having countermanded the delivery of the supplies. This story had been contrived by Ampudia himself, and the dissembling miscreant who bore it, thrown in our way to allure us to a certain destruction. The fellow acted his part with a simplicity that baffled the scrutiny of all who examined him.

Chapter III

Having halted, a council of officers was held, in which it was determined to cross the river immediately, and proceeding to Mier, enforce the execution of the requisition. This was absolutely essential to us now, our provisions being entirely exhausted. Leaving a guard therefore of thirty men with the baggage, on the Texas side, we succeeded by four o'clock P.M., in transporting our troops to the opposite shore, and throwing out an advance, moved forward toward the town, some three miles distant. The evening was gloomy and wet, the rain driving furiously in our faces, whilst the gathering obscurity of approaching night, falling upon the wild and naked hills through which we marched, seemed ominous of the ill-starred fortunes awaiting us. At the distance of a mile from the river, we fell in with some mounted look-outs of the enemy, who fled with the utmost precipitation the moment we came in view. Farther on, our advance came up with their out-posts, and drove them in one after another, until we reached the northern bank of the Alcantro, a few hundred yards from the village. When we arrived here, it was nine o'clock at night, and unusually dark. Pausing upon the bank to ascertain our own and the enemy's position, the latter commenced a heavy and continued fire of musketry upon us from the opposite shore, which the distance and increasing darkness rendered wholly ineffectual. Whilst halting here, a strange light being discovered a short distance above us, Colonel Fisher despatched a reconnoitering party to know its meaning. A young man of the detail falling into a gully on the way, fractured an arm and leg so badly, we were compelled to leave a surgeon and ten men with him, in a cabin close by. The next morning, whilst the battle was raging in the town, the Mexican cavalry stationed outside, assailed this cabin, and after three repulses by its gallant inmates, brought a cannon to bear against it, when its occupants were all killed or captured but two, who effected a junction with the main body.

Amid the darkness and a shower of musket-balls, our gallant little band waded the river opposite the town, guided in their passage by the ceaseless blaze of the enemy's musketry. Captain Baker's company, who were stationed a short distance below our point of crossing, succeeded in a slight measure in diverting their fire, but not a gun was discharged from our party, before we reached the beach under the brow of the village. General Green, with a picked company of volunteers, led the advance; the imploring and shuddering alcalde, enclosed in the forward platoon, begging in low and plaintive

tones, (rendered indistinct by the splash on the water, and the whirr of the balls,) to be allowed to fall back to the rear. As this little vanguard silently reached the opposite shore, they approached a heavy Mexican picket undiscovered, till within a few yards' distance, when a discharge almost simultaneous from their deadly rifles, was followed by piercing yells of anguish, that rose high and distinct above the martial strife around. Those of the enemy's picket neither killed nor wounded by this discharge, broke and fled in the utmost disorder, bearing down their officers, who vainly vociferated and resisted their tumultuous flight into the town. Our prisoner, the alcalde, infected by the panic, bounded with the strides of a chamois up the hill, and disappeared in the darkness. The fugitive enemy, shot down by our unerring marksmen wherever they were visible, retreated in dismay from the river; and advancing with a steady pace up the bank, we drove them into the village. Rallied in the houses, they fired from the windows and parapet walls of the roofs, raking the streets in every direction from the public squares with incessant discharges of artillery. By these latter we lost a single soldier, our men passing under cover of walls and alleys through the suburbs, until they gained a lodgment within a hundred yards of the square. Here the firing on our part ceased for the night, prudently resolving to husband our ammunition, nor waste a single shot, until morning's light should reveal us the foe. The enemy on the contrary kept up an uninterrupted discharge of musketry and artillery, for no possible object we could discern, but to distract our attention from their barricades in progress. These were every where thrown up in the streets—passages opened from room to room, and house to house —and scaling-ladders attached to the walls, to facilitate the ascent of reinforcements, for the morrow's busy work of death. When the moon rose, we could see from the loop-holes and windows of the houses we were in, their numerous squads of cavalry careering around the village, obviously intent upon intercepting what we little meditated—an *escape* or *retreat*. The two houses we occupied, were large stone buildings, containing several rooms each, and one story high, with tall grated windows, and fronted each other at the terminus of a principal avenue, leading to the great square in the centre of the place. This square, enclosing an area of something more than an acre, was formed by parallel rows of stone buildings, intersected at each angle by streets diverging through the village. At the northeastern and northwestern debouchures, two six-pounders were stationed, whilst the houses around, and the square itself, were filled with Mexican troops, and a strong reserve stationed beyond the western wall. But for the darkness when we entered, and the overwhelming numbers of the foe, we might have possessed ourselves of houses on the square, where we could have driven the enemy from the town. The population had abandoned the place early in the day, carrying off with them all that was valuable, and taken refuge in the woods some distance from the scene of conflict.

With the first rays of returning light the combat recommenced. Our men had slept but little, as may be imagined; but a plentiful supply of warm bread, jerked meat, and freshly filled water-jars, prepared by the foresight of those whom we expelled from the houses, left us nothing to complain of on the score of refreshments. The Mexicans trained both of their six-pounders to bear upon our quarters, whilst showers of musket-balls came dancing through every aperture in our buildings, with such harmless profusion as provoked expressions of gratitude from our reckless fellows for the seasonable supply of lead. Facing instead of fronting the range of their artillery, their grape-shot and balls rebounded from our houses, doing no further damage than to scale the surface, and glance off down the street. On the other hand, the carnage of our rifles amongst their artillery-men became perfectly frightful. Earnest and emulous contests were repeatedly witnessed in both our houses for the loop-holes and gratings, whence, steadily as at target firing, the murderous marksmen brought down their victims at every discharge.

Round the gun at the nearest angle of the square the dead and desperately wounded were literally heaped in piles. This gun was manned at five o'clock by a full company of artillerists, and at nine it was silenced and abandoned, but five men and the captain being left alive. The flat roofs of the houses, with raised walls near three feet high, were filled with soldiers, whilst the stone spouts projecting from them dripped freely with the crimson shower distilled above. Wherever a Mexican's head was raised above their surface, if but for a moment's reconnaissance, a Texan bullet found a mark, and the hapless victim a grave. Exasperated with this one-sided butchery, the Mexican officers, at the head of their picked battalions, charged us three separate times, pushing the front of their doomed columns bravely up between the houses containing us. Reserving

our fire until they became fairly wedged between us, at one discharge their ranks were swept into eternal night, the survivors recoiling with cries of horror and dismay.

It would be invidious to recount the many deeds of personal intrepidity enacted by our men in the course of this gallant struggle. Their sallies that succeeded the charges of the Mexicans are unparalleled in the annals of modern war, for reckless impetuosity and desperate fury. The fearless Cameron, whose company garrisoned the back yard of one of the houses, being charged by an imposing force of the enemy, after emptying his rifles into their lines, beat off the foe until he could reload, with the *loose stones in the court*. The battle continued to be disputed with the utmost obstinacy on both sides, until near twelve o'clock, M., when, the Mexican fire having almost ceased, General Ampudia sent in a flag by a prisoner, requesting a cessation of hostilities for an hour. This was the more readily acceded to by our commander, the impression being general that the

Mexicans were desirous of surrendering the town, and drawing off their forces unmolested. A message from the Mexican general soon dispelled this illusion. It contained terms of capitulation for us, in lieu of asking it themselves. It represented the Mexican force as amounting to three thousand men, inclusive of the cavalry outside, with abundant supplies of provision and ammunition, hourly expecting a reinforcement, and all the fortified parts of the village in their possession. They demanded our surrender within the hour, or menaced us with a renewal of the fight, and ultimate unsparing destruction. The terms proposed us were as liberal as could be expected, and the most solemn assurances offered they would be strictly observed.

The question of a rejection or compliance with this demand, was warmly debated by both men and officers. The preponderating force of the enemy—our own diminished supply of ammunition, and destitution of all means to sustain a siege where we were—the hopelessness of a retreat in the face of his fresh and numerous cavalry—inclined many to yield a ready assent to his proposal. Others again were for maintaining our position until night and darkness would lend their protecting aid to a retreat. A third party vehemently urged the prompt evacuation of the town, confronting every hazard, and death, if necessary, sooner than fall into the hands of our implacable foe. Nearly all were united in the determination under no possible circumstances *to abandon the wounded.*

In such gloomy and indecisive discussion the hour of the armistice wore on, and had nearly elapsed, when General Fisher arrived at quarters from a personal interview with Ampudia, strengthened by the Mexican's assurance of safety and good treatment in the policy of a surrender. All extension of time for consideration being denied us, and the utmost disorder beginning to be manifest amongst the men, our commander sorrowfully pressed our immediate capitulation. Here the intrepid Green invited the aid of an hundred volunteers, to cut their way to the Texas camp, or perish in the attempt. The exploit seemed too desperate for success; and, observing Colonel Fisher surrender his sword, and numbers of the men yielding their arms, the frantic soldier shattered his rifle against the ground.

Many were the tears of bitter shame and mortification that coursed down the rugged cheeks of our noble fellows as they marched into the square and stacked their arms. And sadder yet would have beat their hearts, and deeper would the desperation of their lot have smote upon that captive band, had the future unveiled one single scene of the desolate sufferings they were destined to endure.

BOOK II

we were marched some three hundred yards to the entrance of a square yard, surrounded on all sides with high stone walls. Here we defiled into the court, every man being strictly searched as we passed in, and our knives (which we had heretofore been permitted to retain,) taken from us. As one by one we became relieved of our cutlery, we were formed in single file and close rank against two sides of the wall of the square. The Mexican soldiers were also formed by their officers against the remaining sides, in open order and two deep, the rear rank about a pace behind, whilst the entrance through which we had passed was closed with a forest of bayonets. A solemn silence stole over guards and prisoners, occasionally interrupted among the latter by short and husky interrogatories of what the *infernal muster meant?* Hearts amongst our fellows, as lion-like as ever confronted danger, beat with a distinctness almost audible, and eyes that never quailed before at any form of earthly peril, glared with glassy fixedness on the ominous spectacle around. Busy memory turned rapidly over the frightful pages of Mexican perfidy and atrocity, and fancy's fingers, tearing aside the curtain of the past, revealed the sickening tragedy enacted on the gory plains of La Bahia. For the first time the revolting consciousness came over us, we were prisoners, and in the power of Santa Anna, the unscrupulous butcher of Goliad and Bexar. The green graves of six hundred of his soldiers appealed against us for vengeance on their slayers; and who that ever heard of his reckless contempt of faith with friend and foe, but felt how vain the hope to escape his retribution. An hour of torturing uncertainty dragged by, when, with all the gloomy mystery of our coming, we were reconducted to prison. Whatever may have been the purpose of Ampudia, whether to murder or intimidate us, was never disclosed. If the first, the foul deed was averted by an agency inexplicable to us; whilst the latter seemed too pusillanimous and craven for the inherent cruelty and cowardice of Mexicans themselves.

As time wore on, a tale crept in amongst our men, that on the morning after our capture a council of their officers had been held, at which, through the influence of Canales, a verdict of death had been rendered against us. Pursuant to its execution we had been marshalled in the square, and its reversal had only been obtained by Ampudia, through representations of the dictator's displeasure at so flagrant an assumption of his cherished rights of vengeance against all who bore the hated name of Texans. How true or false this version, we will not stop to discuss, since it answered, in the absence of all better explanation, as a clue to the *ghostly* joke.

On the sixth day of our imprisonment at Mier, we were ordered to take up our line of march for Matamoras. None of our men during the campaign had been dismounted for a longer period than a few days; and with the prospect of a pedestrian excursion to the city of Mexico before us, it may be conceived with what sad forebodings of suffering we all set out on foot—save our General and staff. Six hundred infantry, two hundred cavalry, with two six-pounders, and the whole commanded by General Ampudia in person, were deemed the weakest possible escort with which our chivalric victors could safely tempt the highways of their own country, in company with less than two hundred and fifty unarmed prisoners. It was impossible to repress a smile at the mingled pride and caution displayed by this formidable array, in the order of our march.

The swaggering and ragged prisoners, formed in platoons, occupied the centre of an oblong square. On either flank were columns of infantry, and outside of these, files of cavalry. In front was one six-pounder, with artillerymen, cavalry, and the Mexican general and staff; and in the rear, the other piece of ordnance, similarly manned, closed up the cavalcade. It would require the Theban lyrist to portray the firm-paced, slow, and martial step of the whiskered footmen, the pompous ferocity of the fierce hussars, and the triumphal look and stately air of the puissant victor of Mier; who with drums and fife and pealing horns, thundered the renown of his omnipotent arms along the plain.

Leaving our wounded in Mier, with a surgeon and interpreter, a march of twenty-five miles brought us to the village of Camargo. Here, having encamped for the night outside the town, we were early paraded into the village, and compelled to make various circuits of the universal public square, for the entertainment of the citizens, and the glorification of our captors. Being the first specimens of the *espantoso Texanos* that ever appeared in the valley of the Rio Grande, we were regarded by all ages and sexes of these worthy people, with as cautious and severe a scrutiny, as they would have bestowed on the same number of winged griffins. Nor is it easy to decide, whether our vanity or humiliation preponderated, as we looked around upon a multitude assembled from twenty miles' distance, to pay the homage of their guileless curiosity and extorted admiration, to the chastisers of their country's arrogance, and the victors over her invincible tyrant. To be sure we were prisoners, and then undergoing the cruellest adversities of such a lot; but it was equally obvious to all, the fame of our exploits had preceded us, and not a tattered boy of our captive band but imparted more interest to the triumphal pageant, than all the plumed and uniformed cowards exulting in our reverses.

Continuing our route down the river, we reached New Reinosa, some fifty miles distant from Camargo, and halted about two o'clock P.M., on the 4th of January, at the foot of the hill on which the village rests. Here we were met by a despatch from the town, and our guard on receiving it set about adjusting their dress, brushing their accoutrements, and falling into the most becoming and imposing form of procession their ideas of martial grace could suggest. These preparations being concluded, we began the ascent of the hill, and when half way up, were saluted by a straggling discharge of musketry, followed by uncouth yells, that became shriller and more discordant as we approached. Arrived at the top and entering the principal avenue of the town, we passed under an arch of the strangest materials and structure imaginable. A rope stretched *taut* across the mouth of the street, was raised in the centre archlike by an upright pole, and suspended along it in rather tasteful drapery, were fabrics of every hue and texture that the ingenious hand of art ever brought from the loom. Shawls, veils, scarfs, kerchiefs, ribands, muslins, and laces, blended their chaste tints above a coarse substratum of more decided colours, reflected from every garish material, from a blanket to a petticoat. To the right of the centre, streamed down, half revealed, half disclosed, one of these feminine unmentionables of pink and silver; whilst dangling to the left, at a modest distance, protruded the legs of an officer's breeches, flashing with buttons and lace. As we passed down the streets, at every intersection were arches of similar design; and at windows and from parapets, streamed flags and ensigns innumerable. The balconies were crowded with people; myriads of bright eyes, flashing down upon the triumphal scene; whilst our gallant guard, inspired with the intoxicating rapture of the hour, seemed every moment on the point of *immolating* us, to complete the glory and patriotism of the spectacle.

As we entered the public square another *feu de joie* awaited us, and groups of little Carese Indian boys, fantastically arrayed, skipped before the battalion, dancing and singing in wild and graceful measures. The bells of the village clattered throughout our pro-

47

gress as though they would dash from their axles, and the *vivas* of the multitude went up as though celebrating some mighty national jubilee. After a melodramatic promenade three times round the square as usual, we were quartered for the night in a large unfinished brick building in the suburbs.

The day following, Dr. William M. Shepherd was taken from prison to the town, at the solicitation of a priest, (Ampudia's father confessor,) who, during the battle in Mier, was saved from a rifle levelled at him by one of our men, by the timely interposition of the Doctor. The grateful ecclesiastic knew no bounds to the expression of his gratitude, and loaded his benefactor with more substantial proofs of his kindness in the shape of a horse and money. May the worthy old Padre live a thousand years, secure from Texan bullets, *and all other fatal mischances.*

Chapter V

After a sojourn of two days with our delighted hosts the people of New Reinosa, we separated on the morning of the 6th, after hearing mass in the cathedral performed by the worthy Father. There being no such thing as pews or benches in the churches of Mexico, a two hours' standing upon a cold stone floor, listening to devotional services in an unknown tongue, was rather a sorry preliminary to a march of twenty-five miles. Nor was this or any previous march we had yet made alleviated by the character of our quarters at night, when worn and almost spent with fatigue we reached them. A coural (a picketed enclosure for herding sheep, horses, or cattle) was invariably our dormitory since leaving Mier, with the solitary exception of the two nights spent at Reinosa. Every ranch along the road possessed one of these luxurious accommodations. Our guard appropriated the first one that came to hand at the close of day, and driving us into it with as little ceremony as the proprietor would observe towards its legitimate tenants, his stock, we were left to pick the softest heaps of manure on which to repose our wearied bodies. At these places, we despatched the only two meals allowed us during the day. These morning and evening collations consisted for the most time of boiled beef alone; bread or vegetables being very rarely allowed to enliven the solitude of this jealous staple. In a general sense, however, Ampudia's deportment towards us was as liberal as could be expected; his own soldiers sharing our discomforts, and participating in all the deprivations to which we were subjected.

As we approached Matamoras, the country assumed a more beautiful aspect; the rolling prairies were dressed in rich and nutritious muskeet grasses, thickly studded with timber, and filled with numerous herds of fine-looking cattle, the property of more wealthy and substantial farmers than those we had passed above.

Arrived within a few miles' distance of the town, we were halted as usual, for the guard to perform their preparatory toilet. Muskets, swords, and pistols, were again purified of all spots and discolorations, and rubbed until they shone with the brightest refulgence. The cavalry groomed their horses, and officers and men adorned their persons with every article of finery they possessed or could borrow. No volunteer company in the American States were ever more regardful of their appearance at a Fourth of July fête, than were these heroes of Mier on the present occasion. As to our valiant selves, it seemed the force of contrast was most carefully studied, and rigidly preserved. Whilst our guard were as bright and flamingo-like as lace and feathers could make them, the cellars of St. Giles would be desperately put to it to muster a more ragged and Billy Barlow turn-out than we exhibited.

With such a grouping of lights and shadows, the procession moved on. Miles from the city, we were met by crowds of men, women, and children, come out to anticipate their less enterprising friends in getting a first glimpse of the wonderful spectacle. Little squat donkeys, scarce taller than Newfoundland dogs, brought pairs of long-legged fellows, who found it difficult to give their extremities a curl that would keep them from the ground. *Arrieros* (muleteers), with mules strung with inquisitive boys, sent out by their indulgent mammas to satiate their impatient frenzy to see the *Texanos*; nasty-looking women with *tortillas* and fruits for sale; curates, blacklegs, and *leperos*, with several odd and old-fashioned vehicles, whose occupants, from their dress, seemed to belong to the better orders, made up the motley concourse that swarmed round us, front, flank, and rear. Thus escorted, we entered the city of Matamoras, amidst flying banners and a flourish of music. Lines of soldiers were stationed on either side of the street, glittering in burnished armour; whilst gay cavaliers, on spirited *mustangs*, with flowing manes and tails, caracoled before us, almost checking our advance by their numbers and curiosity. As at Reinosa, the balconies, windows, and terraces were filled with well-dressed spectators, and the pavements underneath hived with the lower orders of the population.

Many of these last hissed at us as we passed, with a venomous malice and hate, that would have extorted a largess amongst them from their scapegallows master, could he have witnessed their display of loyalty. Amongst these swarthy, ill-visaged beggars, we not unfrequently noted the ebony visages of runaway slaves from Texas, who find refuge and protection from the philo-negrists of this place. Several of these rascals were recognised by our men as the property of friends at home; and in the interior of Mexico, half the regiments on duty contain more or less of them. Amidst arches with national devices, and flags emblazoned with complimentary mottoes to the all-conquering Ampudia, we were conducted to the ubiquitous square, which having circuited three times with pompous formality, we were led off to our quarters in the suburbs, and rewarded for our docility during the exhibition, by a very tolerable dinner.

During the week we remained in Matamoras, we were treated with marked humanity by all the better classes of population, native and foreign. The military not only supplied us most abundantly with wholesome and palatable food, but the citizens generously contributed large supplies of clothing, which we greatly needed. These donations came from the foreign merchants and Mexican gentry in equal proportions; the ladies, ever foremost in the blessed ministrations of charity, sending us various sums of money in addition to their other bounties.

The noble and devoted generosity of a German merchant, by the name of Schatzell (J. P. Schatzell), deserves not only the lasting gratitude of every member of our unfortunate corps, but the admiration and esteem of every lover of humanity throughout the world. This generous stranger, as soon as he could obtain admission to us, promptly provided for our immediate necessities; and when these were alleviated, in place of leaving our future lot to the precarious bounty of an enemy's alms, distributed the sum of near three thousand dollars in money amongst such as necessity compelled to accept his benevolence. With no solitary claim of country, kindred, or acquaintance, to excite his compassion; captured during an invasion of his adopted country, and fresh from the slaughter of six hundred of its soldiery; he saw in our destitution and distress a field for his Samaritan labours, and regardless of all but our sufferings, divided his store of worldly treasure amongst us, with no hope or security for its return, but the honour and gratitude of the beneficiaries. The American consul called, with others, at our prison; but we are ignorant if further indebted to the interest or humanity of that official.

Amongst the various indulgences extended us, permission to write home to our friends was the most gratifying; and numbers gladly availed themselves of it. This privilege was another of the supernumerary kindnesses of the noble-hearted Schatzell, at whose solicitation it was accorded, and who further took charge of, and securely transmitted our letters. A Texan negro, (Sawney,) became almost an habitué of our prison here; conciliating our esteem by unintermitted acts of service and protestations of kindness, whose treacherous purport was in time revealed to us.

It may not be considered out of connexion here to remark, that whilst we write (October 1844), the citizens of New Orleans have held public meetings, and collected and remitted (with their usual liberality) large supplies for the relief of the people of Matamoras, whose city has just been laid in ruins by a hurricane. This too, whilst their government and Mexico may almost be said to confront one another with drawn swords, upon the irritating questions involved in the annexation movement. No doubt among these sufferers to whom this opportune American succour will be extended, many will be included who little thought at the time of their magnanimous humanity to our distressed fellows, the future held so speedy a requital in store for them. The just providence of Him who holds the destinies of men and communities in his hands, rarely permits an action of disinterested benevolence from either, to go wholly unrewarded.

The object of our long detention in Matamoras was alleged to be the want of specific instructions from the capital with regard to our disposal. Amongst the written stipulations entered into between Ampudia and Fisher, the Mexican had solemnly pledged himself to use his utmost influence with Santa Anna to prevent our being sent to the prisons in the interior. Several of the Santa Fé prisoners, who had been liberated in the preceding June, had joined our expedition, and spread among us such frightful tales of the rigours and horrors of these shambles, that without some agreement on this head, not a man amongst us would have acceded to the surrender. To our consternation an order was received from the Dictator, and communicated to us on the 13th, by Ampudia, directing our immediate march to the capital. It was of little use to murmur or remonstrate, and whatever were our previous hopes, we now gloomily steeled ourselves for the worst fate fortune had in store for us. Of Ampudia (whose command and escort terminated at Matamoras) we had nothing to complain of, that might not have been far worse, had we fallen into the hands of any other of their commanders. This General has since stained his reputation by the cowardice exhibited in his cruelties and indignities to the unfortunate Santamat at Tobasco. But the worst feature of his character that came under our observation, was his silly vanity, which, drunk with the glory of our capture, led him to subject us to impertinent and indelicate exhibitions, that a brave and generous foe would have scorned to impose. Our fare, and the miserable bivouacs assigned us on our march from Mier, rather sprung from the vile condition of the Mexican commissariat, than any meditated neglect of his. And he and his followers having shared these privations, vindicated them from the imputation of wantonly inflicting them.

Leaving Lieutenant Crittenden and five others sick at Matamoras, and three boys, detained by Ampudia under a promise of being set at liberty, we set out for the city of Mexico, on the 14th of January, under a new guard, commanded by General Canales.

This guard consisted of five hundred men, (four hundred infantry and one hundred cavalry, with a field piece,) all new levies, and with none of the discipline and soldierly bearing of those from whose custody they had taken us. It is an old and most correct observation, that the rawer the recruit, the more insolent and brutal is he in his intercourse with all under him or in his power. Not a dog of this guard who did not scowl upon us with all the cowardly malice of bigoted hate, and practise every annoyance toward us that his mingled sense of discipline and apprehensions from ourselves, brought within the scope of impunity. The character of Canales we were familiar with before, and knew that every severity he could exercise on the way, that would fall short of exciting us to open resistance, would be certain to be inflicted. We were, therefore, not wholly unprepared for the inconveniences and petty tyrannies we endured from him and his felon recruits. One security from him we relied on, and that was his fear. This he openly manifested before setting out, in refusing to take charge of us, unless we were *all first ironed*. To so brutal a proposition Ampudia opposed his prompt and decided opposition; and the sneaking poltroon recompensed himself for his baffled cruelty by maintaining, through his subalterns, the most irksome police over us, himself never venturing nearer our lines during the march than a hundred yards. To such excess did he carry his caution, that frequently on the march, when it was necessary for him to pass from the rear to the front of the division, his circuit of us would extend a half mile to the right or left.

Our officers, Colonel Fisher, Major Murray, General Green, and Captain Lyons, with Doctor Shepherd and Daniel Henry, had set out three days in advance of us, having all been rigidly interdicted from any intercourse with the men, save for a few minutes at a time, since the morning of our surrender. In such a separation our vigilant enemy believed he had full guarantees against any attempt on our part at escape, very illogically assuming, that without the co-operation and counsel of our leaders, we would not dare the responsibility of assailing the soldiers surrounding us. However indispensable to such a movement by Mexican soldiers their general and staff might be deemed, a moment's reflection would have taught him, that among Texans no man accounts himself a soldier who is not ever more ready to lead than to follow, in any enterprise of danger.

Chapter VI

*Route from Matamoras · Knavery of the
Mexican commissariat · Scarcity of provisions
and water · Arrival at Sacata · Plan for assailing the
guard · How prevented · Arrival at Catareta ·
Beauty of the town · Our reception · Mexican
oration · Supply of delicacies · Doctor
Bullock · Present of tobacco.*

Leaving Matamoras, our route bore off for a few days in a northwesterly direction, through a level and fertile valley, interspersed with numerous beautiful ponds and lakes. We then struck the ascent to the central plains, or table-lands of Mexico, and continued our march at stages varying from twenty-five to thirty-five miles a day, until having completed a distance of near two hundred miles, we reached the little village of Sacata, on the river San Juan.

Such of us as were unprovided with money during this time, were almost entirely dependent upon our comrades who had it, for the proper amount and quality of food necessary to sustain us in our severe marches. The Mexican commissary received from his government twenty-five cents per diem, for the subsistence of the prisoners; of which amount not five cents a man was expended upon us. The money was properly and legally payable by this functionary to the prisoners in specie; but the commutation was insisted upon by the officer, and the knavery practised upon us as described. Spoiled sea-bread had been laid in at Matamoras to a large amount, which being after various trials positively rejected by the men, was substituted by meagre rations of the cheapest flour to be obtained. And two meals a day of this, with refuse beef, to be cooked as we could best prepare it, without utensils or a sufficiency of firewood, was the provision for our support, whilst undergoing marches that would have worn down well-fed men.

Frequent opportunities were presented to those with money, in

passing the ranches, to lay in supplies, which were improved whenever permitted; and by a generous division of the food so acquired,
the weak and destitute were enabled to sustain themselves. Water,
so difficult to be procured in several arid districts over which we
passed, we were often without for ten and fifteen hours at a time,
being refused the privilege of stopping for it when it was convenient
and directly in the way. At night, our quarters were invariably the
coural of the farm-house at which we tarried; where, midst filth,
and cold, and rain, we were left to recruit our strength for the next
day's recurring trial. It will not be supposed that men unused to
these trials of suffering, would quietly and unrepiningly submit to
them. The act of our liberation had been the standing topic of discussion, from the hour of our surrender; and notwithstanding the
surveillance maintained over us, we found abundant opportunity to
mature our plans, and resolved on their execution whenever the
auspicious moment should present itself. The captains of our six
companies were with us, and to them was deputed the task to select
the place, the hour, and the mode, for the achievement of our freedom. Every mile we advanced into the interior increased the difficulties and hazards of our escape, without in the least degree relax-
ing the vigilance of our guard. It had been determined, therefore,
that the first encampment we made propitious to our designs,
should be the scene of our emancipation, or immolation. We arrived
early in the evening at Sacata, and were as usual turned into a coural
in the suburbs. The cavalry were picketed in equal numbers, on the
left and rear of our pen. The infantry occupied the right and front;
their line in front extending from the gate of the coural some one
hundred and fifty yards, to the six-pounder, which, loaded and pointed at the only outlet to the place, was surrounded by the artillery-
men, (a burning match near at hand,) ready for use at a moment's
warning. Captain E. Cameron, a Scotchman by birth, and as heroic
a soldier as ever buckled sword around him, was by general consent
assigned the command, and the task of giving the signal for the onset. Our men were divided into four companies, and to each was allotted a particular duty. Right and left, front and rear, the enemy
were to be assailed at the same moment; whilst the capture of the
gun, deemed of paramount importance, was confided to a select few
of the most able-bodied and desperate amongst us. The signal agreed
upon, and to be communicated by Cameron, was the command of
draw; it being the usual order issued for forming the men, to re-

ceive their rations, morning and evening. The attempt was esteemed by all one of imminent hazard; the conflict to follow a sanguinary one, and the result doubtful; yet all seemed resolved upon it, cost what it would, and eventuate as it might.

About four o'clock, the time for the delivery of our supper arrived. The persons bearing the provisions, with the asses loaded with the fuel, were seen approaching the coural. The men were formed, and the hazard of life and death, liberty and slavery, hung suspended upon the utterance of the terrible signal. Outside of the enclosure could be seen the glittering muskets, stacked in tempting piles; whilst the unconscious guard were lolling at their ease, smoking, gossiping, or sleeping, as their various humours or inclinations invited. Every eye in our desperate battalion seemed riveted with the potency of fascination, upon the towering and athletic Cameron; whose own were bent in turn with the calmness of fate, upon the approaching troop of servitors, who were already entering the coural. *Draw your rations first*, was the ambiguous signal that saluted our ears, delivered in the commonplace tone of daily custom, and unattended by a single demonstration or look, explanatory, beyond the simple counsel it implied. The men looked bewildered—hesitated—gazed out over the pickets as apprehending a discovery of the plot, and some certain precautions for its defeat; then looked at Cameron again, who was busily engaged with his supper. In a moment more they were all similarly absorbed in the base employments of baking, roasting, and gorging.

A portion of Cameron's company, to whom he was devotedly and blindly attached, had appealed successfully, on the spur of the moment, for the postponement of the enterprise; and relying upon no man's budging in the adventure, without the signal as agreed upon, he had adopted this hazardous but successful means, of frustrating its present execution. Such was his explanation afterwards, and however strange and incredulously it was at first received, but a few days elapsed before he was acquitted of all blame or dishonour for balking the attempt.

Three days' march from Sacata, brought us to Catareta, the most beautiful village within the confines of Mexico. Perched upon an emerald knoll, swelling gently up from the river San Juan, which girds its base, its miniature fortifications, steeples, towers, and surrounding gardens, lent it a witchery of look, that sunk upon all our souls with the magic of a fairy spell. It seemed we were not entirely

unexpected either, as a band of delicious music met us at the water's edge, and in strains of enchanting harmony, welcomed us through its massive archway. Its bells rung out their sweetest peals, whilst numerous rockets careering through the air, kindled the very atmosphere above into a luminous blaze. In the midst of its marble square, a murmuring fountain sung untiring lullabies; and lofty pyramids distributed around, held groups of youthful pyrotechnics, as jocund and brilliant as the sparkling messengers they sent up. Fronting a rostrum overhung by a raised pavilion, was assembled a gay and holiday multitude, listening to an orator, who, in the purest Castilian, and with the most graceful elocution, was there to welcome and congratulate our party.

The address being especially dedicated to our improvement and instruction, the attentive guard disposed us in a manner to listen with the utmost advantage to the discourse. The exordium, which was progressing as we entered, was a rehearsal of the power, fame,

and civilization of the august republic we were visiting; with vivid and flattering allusions to the devoted love of freedom, justice, and humanity, so characteristic of its brave and enlightened citizens. The order, beauty, and benignity of their government; the admiration it excited abroad amongst the less fortunate nations of the earth; the veneration, happiness, and security it preserved at home, by the liberality and impartiality of its administration; were so brilliantly and earnestly managed by the speaker, as to elicit frequent and prolonged *vivas* from his delighted auditors. But if he seemed animated and fired by the civic blessings so bountifully heaped upon his favoured land, how shall be described the rapt and burning inspiration of his tone, look, and accents, when he came to refer to her terrible renown in war, and the glory and lustre of her arms, on the countless battle-fields they had immortalized. From the first exploits of the invincible Cortes in Tlascala, to his decisive victory on Tezcuco; from the club-wrought massacres of the patriot Hidalgo, and his insurrectionary host, down to our late capture by the invincible Ampudia; every successful battle within their dominions, whether won by Guachapin or Aztecs, Creoles or Mestizoes, was extolled in such terms of imposing panegyric and gorgeous rhetoric, as filled the Mexican part of the audience with pride and transport. Our calamities we were assured were the inevitable fate of all whose audacity led them to oppose their resistless arms. Our spared lives were monuments of that godlike clemency with which the great nation was accustomed to temper the severity of its chastisements. We were felicitated on the opportunity we were then enjoying, of becoming familiar with the usages and sentiments of those unalterably decreed to rule over us; and dismissed with a recommendation to maintain our fortitude and submission, and further enjoined to do justice to Mexican humanity and generosity, should it please Heaven and the President to permit us to return home.

This eloquent vindication of Mexican renown, (with the no doubt well-meant admonitions to ourselves,) would have been quite as much in place, had they been couched in the ancient Phrygian tongue, as in liquid Spanish, in which they were delivered. Nineteen twentieths of our fellows being as innocent of any knowledge of the dialect in which we were addressed, as so many Cumanches may be supposed of the idiomatic elegancies of St. Cloud. From a country, however, in which the custom of public speaking is extensively practised, and sacredly respected, they yielded the orator their most flattering and serious attention, and no one who had witnessed their gravity and decorum, but would have inferred they were most critically and acutely absorbed in the argument of the discourse.

Dark mustached men, with shouldered firelocks, enforced these inculcations with scowls of vengeful import; but more persuasive endorsers were there in the bright-eyed daughters of New Leon, whose graceful *rebosos* illy concealed the pity that bedewed their long lashes, as they gazed through the soldiery upon our sad and forlorn-looking files.

When we reached the quarters allotted us by our hospitable hosts of Catareta, we were equally surprised as grieved to find them the open back-yard of the barracks; and incomparably the most filthy and uncomfortable of any we had tenanted inside of a Mexican town. This mole upon the cheek of the village, we felt sure could not have been wittingly selected as our resting-place; after such unbounded manifestations of joy over our arrival, and lively sympathy in our welfare as had been expressed. Rain, too, beginning to fall upon our uncovered heads, we indignantly complained to some respectable citizens standing near; who, after a remonstrance with the brute Canales, prevailed in having us removed to snugger apartments.

Here we were abundantly supplied with hot tortillas, frijoles and fowls, with oranges and various fruits, that are grown in the greatest abundance near this delightful village.

Doctor Bullock, a young and very popular American physician, whose good genius had directed his footsteps to this paradise, which his good taste at once appropriated as a residence, came frequently to see us, and displayed his sympathy and solicitude for our comfort, by every kindness and attention compatible with his means and the license allowed him.

Through him we were enabled to procure a liberal supply of very tolerable tobacco; an article commanding the most exorbitant prices in the region we were in, being exclusively in the hands of contrabandistas when it can be found at all. Had the banquet board of Mexico's most luxurious viceroy spread its appetiting dainties before our men, they would have been cheerfully exchanged by most of them for this grateful godsend of the much-esteemed weed.

A heavy and unintermitted rain detained us in this village through the following day and night; and on the morning of the 28th we resumed our march for the neighbouring city of Monterey.

Chapter VII

The valley of Monterey, or the San Juan, as it is indifferently termed, through which we now pursued our way, is unsurpassed in the world for its fertility, the brilliancy and luxuriance of its vegetation, the salubrity of its climate, and the picturesque character of its scenery. Narrowing as it extends westward, its breadth, for near a hundred miles below Monterey, varies from fifteen to twenty miles, the lands sloping with the most gentle descent from the low mountain on either side to the river. From the sides of these hills burst innumerable springs of the most delicious water, furnishing convenient means of artificial irrigation during the protracted droughts to which these regions are subject. Here, in friendly neighbourhood, are to be found, the oak and pecan tree, the plantain and the orange, the pine-apple and banana, whilst fields of wheat and maize stretch down from the mountain's base, to extended plantations of sugar and maguey.

The latter crops are by far the most profitable of any branches of agriculture pursued in Mexico. The labour of both is conducted by the native Indians, whose wages average something under two reals per day. Many of the sugar estates are reputed to yield above a million of pounds of refined sugar, with molasses sufficient to pay the entire expenses of their cultivation, and the cost of preparing the crop for market. From three to five hundred labourers are employed upon the larger ones, whose wages are still further reduced, by payment in goods and groceries, at enormous prices. The income of their proprietors are thus rendered far more certain, and frequently equal to the most fortunate miners. The cultivation of the maguey, (the Agave Americana,) from whose saccharine juices pulque is made, (the popular drink of the country,) is still more extensively carried on, yielding enormous returns, and being indigenous to every variety of Mexican climate and elevation of soil. Whole tracts of country are to be found where the face of nature presents one unvaried field of this sharp and thorn-leafed plant. The early maturity of its growth varies with its approximation to the seacoast, and occurs at periods ranging from five to as high as twenty years. In the *tierras calientes* (warm lands) it sends up its flowering stem in five or seven years; in the *tierras templados* (middle plains), in from ten to twelve, and in the cold lands (*tierras frias*), it is often as long as twenty years ere it ripens. When flowered, the stalk is often more than a foot in diameter, and twelve to fourteen feet in height. This is tapped, and the interior pulp removed, leaving a hollow bowl, into which, for five and seven months at a time, a honied subacid juice continues to be distilled, whose daily yield, from a thrifty plant, not unfrequently amounts to the enormous quantity of twelve and fifteen pints. The saccharine and mucilaginous properties of this sap provoke a ready fermentation, and the liquor obtained, though nauseous and disgusting at first, is esteemed, by those who overcome this first repulsion, above all other drinks. The Indians, besides being devoted to the flavour of this beverage, regard it as highly medicinal, and use it in their families with more prodigal excess than the populace of London do beer. The brandy, or intoxicating spirit derived from it, is obtained by distillation, and is the fatal agent of the increasing demoralization so steadily advancing amongst the lower orders of the population.

The maguey was not only the vine of the ancient Mexicans, but their hemp and papyrus likewise, their hieroglyphics being mostly painted upon a paper made from its leaves, and the *pita* (a strong and even thread, still highly esteemed and in use amongst them), manufactured from its fibres. Many of the plantations of agave produce a moneyed rent to their absentee lords of from twenty to fifty thousand dollars. These haciendas are seldom tenanted by the proprietors, but left to the management of administradors, the owners residing in the capital of the republic, or the chief city of the state in which the property may happen to lie. The domain annexed to the more respectable of them varies from five to ten leagues in extent, and what with the large and massive dwellings, the surrounding offices, warehouses, mills, work-houses, and Indian villages, they more resemble towns than single plantations.

Continuing our way along the banks of the river that intersects this beautiful valley, crossing and recrossing it at distances of every ten miles, a little beyond the picturesque Mission of Guadaloupe we encountered numerous companies of persons, mounted and on foot, come out from Monterey to get a look at us. They were by far more civil and respectful visiters than we anticipated, scanning our appearance with eager but not offensive curiosity, and escorting us into the city without any manifestation of that vulgar triumph we had experienced from the population of nearly all the towns through which we passed.

Monterey (the city of the mountains) is the capital of New Leon, and amongst the largest towns in eastern Mexico. It is situated on the head waters of the San Juan, between two lofty mountains, built in a style of considerable taste and splendour, and supposed to contain about two thousand inhabitants. Amongst these are the most wealthy and distinguished families of the state, noted equally for the liberality of their opinions, as the elegance and hospitality of their habits.

The region round about is wild and romantic beyond description; bold and rugged hills towering peak above peak, whilst spread out along their base creep wooded and smiling valleys, robed in beauty and adorned with cultivation. At twelve miles' distance, the loftiest summit, fifteen hundred feet high, takes the name of the *Cumanche Saddle*, from its striking resemblance to the peculiar form of that cavalry equipment in use amongst those Indians. To the south, in the same range of hills, is also to be seen the famous Puerto de los Muertos, (or gate of the dead,) being a gloomy gorge or pass in the mountain, through which, alone, from Jalapa to Monterey, wheeled carriages can ascend from the coast to the table-land.

During our residence of three days in Monterey, our quarters were as comfortable as could be provided, and rations the very best to be procured. We further received, as proofs of sympathy and benevolence, presents of shoes and sandals, with various articles of clothing, that confirmed our previous estimate of the humanity and kindness of its citizens.

Here, to our great delight, Canales surrendered his further command over us to Colonel Baragan, an accomplished and humane officer, and as unlike his predecessor as courage and generosity ever differ from cowardice and cruelty. Our infantry guard was also changed and greatly reduced; the substitutes consisting for the most part of fresh conscripts, many of them taken from the prisons of Monterey, barely familiar with the rudiments of the service, and destitute of all pride or honour so indispensable to the composition of good soldiers.

Nothing could enchant us more highly than this change of the guard; holding out as it did the hope of a more successful liberation on the road.

Descending again into the beautiful valley of the Monterey, we continued up the river, passing through unfenced plantations on our route, walled in on either side by parallel ranges of mountains, that from crag and cavern flung back the strains of our bugles in a thousand weird and mocking echoes.

A march of thirty miles brought us to Rinconada, a large ranch near the river San Juan, running up for several thousand acres into a cove of the mountains. Here we once more determined to disarm our guard, the situation of the camp favouring the design, and men and officers alike concurring in the feasibility of the plan.

The quarters allotted us for the night consisted of three connected courts or pens, separated by mud walls some six feet high, and opening into each other by gateways, closed by poles or bars. The first was occupied by the infantry, the second by our men, and the third to the rear of us, by the cavalry. At daybreak the following morning we were quietly awakened by our leaders, and every man quickly at his post, ready for the work. This hour had been agreed upon, as the cavalry it was supposed would be out in the plain collecting their horses, and hopes were entertained we should find the infantry asleep, and easily dispersed or taken as soon as we secured their arms. The sudden roll of the Mexicans' drums in the adjoining pen dissipated in a moment our cherished hopes of freedom, and, looking into their quarters, we discovered the whole guard filing out of the coural, and forming in order for march. This was too unusual an evolution to leave us in a moment's doubt but that our plan had been discovered, and fairly anticipated, by the vigilance of the enemy.

How he obtained his information was never conclusively ascertained, but the strongest circumstances conspired to excite suspicion against the negro Sawney. This fellow had joined us at Matamoras, and, affecting to belong to the Mexican army, had the *entrée* to our quarters at all times, sharing liberally in the confidence of several of our men, from his professed devotion and attachment to their interests. Several of the prisoners who had opposed the outbreak as too desperate and unequal for success, likewise fell under suspicion of having denounced it to Baragan; but reason and reflection soon acquitted them of the unworthy charge, leaving the imputation to rest upon the perfidious slave, to whom alone it is believed to be due.

On Sunday, the 5th of February, we entered Saltillio, a neat and populous city, of some ten thousand inhabitants, situated in the extreme southern part of Coahuila, and on the head waters of the San Juan. The grounds in its immediate vicinity, with the numerous gardens of the city, are irrigated by beautiful fountains of water, springing up in various parts of the town. The valley here is broad and filled with the most luxuriant herbage, whilst at no great distance to the north, rise dreary mountains from the midst of desolate and barren-looking plains. Such contrasts of mountain and meadow, fertility and barrenness, beauty and deformity of landscape are frequent in the Northeastern States of Mexico; every diversified aspect of soil and production being found grouped within the narrowest compass. An antique and massive-looking church adorns the public square of Saltillio, and many private residences of size and pretension, indicate a high degree of opulence and taste in the owners. Here our guard was strongly reinforced, leaving no further room to doubt that our designs against them were well understood, and properly provided against.

After resting two days we resumed our march, bearing south, in the direction of San Luis Potosi, over a rugged and mountainous country, thinly populated, and entirely destitute of water, save at long distances, where it is preserved in tanks, for the relief of travellers. Precipitous and almost naked hills, with sides ploughed into deep ravines, nod over valleys as arid and inhospitable as themselves; whilst the scattering *ranches* reared midst their defiles are tenanted by a poor and bandit-looking race, who draw a precarious subsistence from the miserable shelter and mean entertainment they furnish the wayfarer. At one of them, (*Agua ebuebo*,) at which we rested during our first night from Saltillio, we were shown this room where the brave and unfortunate Captain Dimitt, of Texas, poisoned himself; all his comrades being overtaken and killed by the guard but two.

On our fourth day's march through these dismal solitudes, we arrived early in the evening of the 10th inst., at the ranch Salado, where weary, worn, and disgusted with captivity, we determined to achieve our liberty, or perish in the effort. No sooner therefore were we penned, than Doctor Brenham, Doctor M'Math, Judges Gibson and Walker, ever foremost in counselling this daring step, renewed their opposition to its further postponement; and after finding a large majority of the prisoners disposed for its immediate execution, arranged the rising for the following morning, whatever might betide. As night approached, it became evident the Mexican colonel was fully apprised of some mischief brewing in our quarters. The sentries were doubled, their guns examined, discharged and reloaded; and every precaution taken to insure against surprise that vigilance and prudence could suggest. Despite it all, we lay down to rest, resolved that the morning's sun should light us to freedom, or go down upon our graves.

Chapter VIII

*Our quarters · Distribution of the
detachment · Attack on the guard · Killed,
wounded, prisoners, and spoils · Interview with
Colonel Baragan · Appearance of our men on the
march · Thoughts of home · Fired on from a
ranch · Meet with a friend · His counsel ·
Refused provisions at ranches · Conduct
on the road · Retreat to the mountains.*

The Salado is situated in a sterile sandy valley, of considerable extent, almost barren of vegetation, and as desolate in appearance as could well be selected for the habitation of man. This ranch differs in nothing from the usual style of such buildings, save in the comfortless character of its arrangements, and the absence in the surrounding landscape of any solitary feature to enliven the general gloom of its aspect. It is one hundred and twenty miles from Saltillio, and was kept as a posada at the time, by a smut-faced, ill-visaged Mexican, who let its vile accommodations to such travellers between Saltillio and San Luis Potosi, as extremity drove to take refuge with him. A quadrangular stone court, embracing the main buildings of the ranch, with thick walls ten feet high, constituted the quarters of the infantry part of our guard. Connected with it by similar walls, and communicating with it by a large doorway, was the coural in which we were confined. The cavalry were picketed outside, in such manner as to surround three sides of the coural. Our plans being matured, and a thorough understanding subsisting amongst our men, Captain Cameron was again appointed to give the signal, and all lay down to refresh them with a sleep.

Between daylight and sunrise every man was up receiving his breakfast of boiled rice, and seemingly as intent in discussing it, as though not a thought beyond was permitted to disturb the keenness of his appetite. From a sunken part of the wall between the coural and the court-yard, four sleepy-looking sentinels with ground arms, were standing at ease; whilst the two patrols on the outside of the doorway (the only outlet from our pen) were leaning on their muskets, and looking in upon our noisy voracity, with a mingled expression of commiseration and disgust. Our neighbours in the court were all awake; some busy with their own breakfast, some stowing away their blankets, and others grouped near the gate, holding a *tête-à-tête* with the cavalry outside. It was a curious spectacle for one in the humour for such observation, to have watched the strained and fascinated concentration of our men's eyes, as they peered from below the slouched ruins of their hats and caps, upon the *nonchalant* and unintelligible movements of the *chief conspirator.*

Tranquilly, and with an air of vulgar relish, he continued to munch his gourd of rice, as he advanced with a careless and loitering step nearer and nearer the doorway of the coural. Arrived within a few paces of the sentries, and having stared with a vacant look into the court beyond, he suddenly faced about, and in a voice that rung through the whole ranch, shouted the concerted signal, *"Now, boys, we go it!"*

With the bounds and cries of unleashed bull-dogs, our men dashed through the doorway into the court, and seizing the muskets stacked against the side of the wall, turned them upon the panic-stricken and flying guard. This was the work of a moment; scarce ten guns being fired ere the yard (of late so populous with heroes), was empty of Mexicans, save the trembling and supplicating sentries, who were first knocked down and disarmed. Two only of the enemy were killed here, and a few wounded. A part escaped into the plain, and the rest took refuge in the adjacent houses. The officers and a few cavalry soldiers, discharged their pistols and carbines from these buildings and fled. One of our men fell desperately wounded from this volley, and died a few hours after.

Outside, a company of infantry had rallied, and being joined by some fifty mounted men, seemed disposed to tarry our coming. The intrepid Brenham and Lyons (both released Santa Fé prisoners) in heading the *sortie* out of the court, were shot down in the gateway by Mexicans sheltered in the buildings to the left. The enemy then fled at our approach, without firing a shot; and through the plain and *capperel* as far as the eye could range, his dispersed and panting platoons might be seen scampering towards opposite points of the

horizon, as though legions of armed furies were thundering at their heels. The loss on either side was about equal; several of their men, expecting no quarter, being killed in the houses, and the same number of ours being slain or wounded in the stable lot by a party of the enemy who fired on them from the wall. More than a third of their guns that fell into our hands were found empty, and their cartridge-boxes, in place of ammunition, filled with cigars and other soldier-traps. But for this, their speedy flight might not have prevented a more serious loss. The negro Sawney proved more alert in escape than any of his comrades, having, fortunately for himself, vanished with the first sound of the tumult.

Our killed were, Brenham, Lyons, Fitzgerald, Rice, and Hagerty; wounded, Captain Baker, Hancock, Harvey, Sansbury, and Trahern. All our prisoners were dismissed unharmed; amongst whom were several officers, who were permitted to retain their swords. Colonel Fisher and staff, who were in the ranch during the night, started with their escort before daybreak, and distinctly heard our hurras at the conclusion of the affair, although we were ignorant of their vicinity.

Pursuant to the example of the most renowned victors on record, we first celebrated our triumph with three times three loud and hearty cheers, then set about collecting and examining the spoils.

An hundred and sixty muskets and carbines, with some dozen swords and pistols, and three mule-loads of ammunition, were our most important trophies. Near a hundred mules and horses were our next most valuable acquisition. A plentiful supply of provisions, and fourteen hundred dollars in cash, (government funds,) were also forgotten in the hurry of the enemy's departure. Taking possession of these, with such a portion of the provisions as we could conveniently transport, and leaving our sick and wounded with some twenty eccentric knights of our party, who refused to accompany us, confiding in the idle hopes of an early release; we appointed the gallant Cameron to the command, and commenced a retrograde march over the line of route we pursued in coming.

Colonel Baragan, who had done every thing that a brave and devoted officer could do to check the flight of his men, and had been himself the last hostile Mexican on the field, now presented himself about half a mile down the road, with a few cavalry he had rallied, and requested on our approach to communicate with us. He seemed deeply chagrined at our escape, and doubtless anticipated the heavy censure from his superiors it was destined to bring upon him. Through his interpreter he remonstrated against the madness of the step we had taken; pointing out the impossibilities of our hopes, and reminding us of his uniform clemency and humanity, invoked our submission, promising an amnesty for what had passed, and assurances of every possible kindness in the future.

With unaffected regret at parting with this generous officer, we were compelled to decline his very flattering proposals, lamenting at the same time, that our freedom had not been purchased without detriment or sacrifice to himself. With an expression of genuine thanks to him for the liberality of his treatment of us, we took a courteous leave of him and his little troop, and pursued our way. In this, however, Colonel Baragan did not imitate our magnanimity, but hung upon our rear during the day and night, keeping us steadily in view, and tracking us for several succeeding days through the mountains, signalling our whereabouts, and lending the most important aid to our subsequent recapture.

There was something picturesque, brigandish, and barbaric, in the *ensemble* of our battalion, as it wound its straggling way through the dark and goblin-looking region through which we marched. About half our men were mounted, some very strong mules carrying double. Officers on horseback, in rags and sandals, armed with musket, sword, and pistols; and privates on foot in richly-worked zerapes, sporting long lances, whose glistening shafts resembled at a distance the gilded rods of ushers. The low crowned, broad-brimmed, oil-covered Mexican sombrero, was seen side by side in earnest discourse with some towering hatless grenadier, whose long and matted locks hung down from underneath the crimson kerchief, bound tightly round his crown. Dark, bushy-bearded men, showed arms and legs like circus Athletæ, protruding from knee and elbow, through the short jackets and open breeches of the country's fashion. Here a one-skirted coat, and there no coat at all. Here an officer's saddle and caparisons richly embossed, and mounted with silver; and there a sheepskin, flung over a gay-looking horse, ridden with a lariat bridle.

But we were free once more; and though far from friends and succour, and in the heart of the foeman's land, with his bloodhounds at our heels; many were the hymns of home and country that burst from our exulting lips, and scared with their jovial echoes the startled wild-bird from its perch. When the moon came out to set her watch in the sky, and star by star climbed up to its burning throne, we halted on the mountain summit to scan the jewelled host, and search amongst its radiant galaxies for that lone and new-born gem, that mirrored the stainless flag of Texas.

It was twelve o'clock at night when we stopped to refresh ourselves at the ranch Incarnation; where, having eaten and baited our horses, (paying scrupulously for all we took,) we continued our march until daylight next morning, when we camped, having travelled near seventy miles. Our men walked and rode alternately, relieving each other with the utmost alacrity, and sustaining their fatigues with a cheerfulness inspired by a sense of freedom, and that fortitude and courage needed to insure their arrival at home. Home! and what visions of bright and glowing happiness does not this necromantic word bring up in the waking or dreaming thoughts of all, who have ever known its spells. How its dull cares and active sorrows, its chilling penury and freezing neglect, its actual outlawry, all soften down in absence before the memory of one loved look or tone, and dissolving into hues of hope and tenderness, disperse the shadows from the heart, like the gleam of blessed tapers above holy shrines. Such images nerve the soul and paint the dreams of mariner and soldier, amidst wreck and hostile perils; but who can colour their enchantment to him, who has just broke the sullying chain, and flung off the captive's crushing load!

Our stiffened limbs were allowed but slight repose from the toils of the preceding day, ere we were once more on the march. At the distance of some twenty miles we turned off from the road to the left, and entered a gorge of the mountain, embowered in a forest of palmettoes. Through this wood the feet and legs of our men who walked, were wounded at every step, by the sharp thorn of the wild maguey, and innumerable spinous shrubs, that choked up the way. Emerging at length into the open valley, bleeding and consumed with thirst, (having tasted no water for twenty hours,) we hastened towards a ranch just visible in a distant curve of the valley, where we hoped to procure a supply. When within two hundred yards of the enclosure, what was our surprise to see the house-top bristling with the lances of the cavalry, and the windows stuck full of the muzzles of their carbines. At so manifest a determination to sell us the desired relief only at the price of bloodshed, we filed off towards the north, in the direction of a gap in the mountains, preferring a further search to rousing the country by any unnecessary violence.

As we turned from them, the garrison fired a volley over our heads, accompanied by loud exultations, that required all the authority our officers could exert, to prevent being returned. The audacity of these scouts rendered it clear we were closely trailed, and active preparations in progress for our recapture. On the opposite side of the mountain our advance found a sufficiency of water, which, after greedily swallowing, and filling our gourds, we continued our march to the north. Several hours' travel brought us to a sequestered ranch, where, having halted and interrogated its inmates of our whereabouts, we wheeled to the west, and pursued our route over a level sandy plain, thickly studded with capperel.

It was in vain we sought to elude the vigilance of the foe. Turn to what point of the compass we might, not an hour elapsed before the smoke of his signal-fires was seen to curl from some eminence in our front. Leaving the plain as the sun descended, we again entered the mountains, to find a favourable spot on which to encamp. Having rested through the night, we resumed our march at daylight, with a Mexican guide, who had entered our camp the previous night, and readily volunteered to direct us. Two of our men wandered off and were lost on the preceding night, and another left asleep at this camp. We continued to the westward until we struck the Monclova road, and had not pursued it far, before we were hailed by an American friend, who, on hearing of our escape, had despatched us the guide then with us, instructed to conduct us to the spot where he lay concealed to receive us. From him we learned that expresses from Baragan had carried intelligence of our *break* to every ranch and town within two hundred miles west and north of the Salado; that no adequate force was as yet raised to pursue us, but that our safety depended upon expedition, as the country was in the greatest alarm at the news of our being at large, and would promptly organize to follow and retake us. He further impressed it upon us to keep the road we were then pursuing, and under no pretext whatever to deviate from it until beyond the pass of Benado. Commending his guide again to us as important and trustworthy, with a thousand earnest prayers for our safety and escape, this noble fellow took his leave, and disappeared in the thicket.

During the evening we passed two respectable and comfortable-looking ranches, at which we in vain essayed to purchase a supply of corn and beef. As we approached them, the gates were barred, the doors all fastened, and a red flag hung out, to indicate the hostility of the proprietors. These obstinately refused to open any commerce with us, but bade us pass on, which request they fortified by a flourish of rusty firelocks, and multiplied disguises of the same head at the windows, to suggest the presence of a formidable force within doors. Our resolution being fixed to practise no violence or rapine on the people, unless in the greatest extremity or self-defence, we continued our way without molesting them. Grazing our horses in the evening near the last of these ranches, our guide, who had been sent in to negotiate for provisions, was detained by the inmates, nor missed until we had advanced some distance on the road.

It was near twelve o'clock at night, and whilst on the march, that a hurried consultation was held by the officers, in which it was madly determined to leave the road and take refuge in the adjacent mountains. This step, against which we had been so solemnly admonished, and which was destined to result in such suffering and disaster to us, had its origin in the apprehension of a minority of the men, who adhered to it with such obstinacy and determined pertinacity as forced its adoption by the majority, who were compelled to acquiesce with them, or consent to a division of the force.

Despite the assurances of our friend, that we were not, and could not be pursued immediately, by a detachment large enough to recapture us, the alarms of these men could be tranquillized by no argument short of an immediate covert in the hills. To separate from them was to insure the certain destruction of all (our present number barely reaching two hundred); and, adopting the only alternative left us, to share their fortunes, we struck abruptly into the thicket, and encamped.

BOOK III

Chapter IX

*Mountains of Coahuila · Fired on by
Mexican scouts · Horrors of our situation ·
Find water · Butcher horses and mules · Comrades
who give out · Fruitless search for water · Famine and
thirst · Descend from the mountains · Sufferings ·
Recapture by Mexicans · Reception in camp ·
Officers · March for Saltillio · Order for our
execution · Refusal of General Mexier
to obey it · Marched into town.*

The wild and rugged-looking mountains that rose before us on the following morning, were so savage, dreary, and seemingly interminable in their outline, as to infuse a visible dejection into the minds of those most clamorous for their protecting shelter. Their rocky sides grizzled over with stunted alpine plants; their naked and sterile peaks destitute of vegetation, save here and there a group of wilted and blasted pines; their gloomy and dismal barrancas, gaping underneath the beetling crags and toppling cones above, frowned repulsively against our meditated intrusion into their stern solitudes.

Some Mexican prowlers, however, having fired upon our camp during the previous night, revived apprehensions of the neighbourhood of the pursuing foe; and up the ascent we went, climbing over projections and picking along precipices, that under other circumstances would have been deemed impossible, to men or animals. Through the tedious day we staggered on from acclivity to acclivity, from hill-top to valley, and from valley to hill-top again; plunging deeper and farther into their lonesome wastes, until night and exhaustion put a period to our toils. Baffled in every attempt to discover a spring or any deposit of water on the eminences, we descended to hunt through the narrow and tortuous valleys as fruitlessly. Not a drop of moisture seemed to exist within the circumference of this arid desolation, though many a deep and yawning gully showed where the tempest had ploughed a path for its torrents, down the hard and impenetrable sides of the mountain. Nor voice of bird nor beast of any kind, broke the frightful silence that reigned throughout, from pinnacle to pit.

Pausing for the night before a perpendicular wall of rock that blocked up all farther progress, our hungry mules limping off in the darkness to search the loose stone and sand for forage, left their spent and tired riders crouching from the bleak night-winds around dismal camp-fires, to ruminate, silent and unsocial, over the *choice*, not *chance*, that brought them there. Sad as looked the present, and disheartening as rose the perspective, but a brief interval elapsed, ere stretched upon their flinty couches, the whole were sunk in sleep. An exploring party who had started betimes in the morning, returned to camp about ten o'clock, with the joyful intelligence of the discovery of water. The cry of land from the masthead, never revived the drooping spirits of a perishing crew, as did this announcement cheer and animate our thirsty band. The two miles interposing between the camp and water, were traversed with the impatience of bridegrooms; and when arrived at the limpid pool, it was found sufficient not only to assuage our present thirst, but fill the gourds of all who had them. Here we moved our camp, and spent the day. Building numerous fires in the little dell, we set about butchering our stiffened horses and mules; barbecuing the flesh over the embers, and each man packing up for future use as much of it as he could conveniently carry. It was thought mercy to them, thus to anticipate the lingering famine and death that awaited them amongst these herbless and naked hills. Our saddles we also cut up and made sandals of; and all our preparations being completed that evening, we set out next day on foot, with heavy packs and heavy hearts. Clambering up the mountain, we directd our course to the north; sometimes along ridges, but for the most of the way, ascending and descending the mountains, from base to summit, and from summit to base again. About four o'clock in the evening of this day, three of our stoutest-looking men, Iseland, Este, and Fitzgerald, gave out, and could go no further; they were supplied with ammunition and meat, their gourds filled with water, and left to shift for themselves. Having travelled until late in the night, a distance (as well as we could reckon) of more than twenty miles, we halted in a ravine, where we had plenty of firewood, and a comfortable shelter from the wind. The next morning when about to resume our march, two others of our men, Miller and Pilley, declared their inability to proceed, and after remonstrance and persuasion had been urged upon them in vain, they were left to their fate. Our plan of getting forward was first to ascend to the ridges, and then steer our course along them as accurately as the nature of the ground admitted of, a due northwestern direction. At the distance of eight miles farther on, Doctor McMath, T. W. Cox, Blackburn, and W. Davis, threw down their packs and bade us adieu, being spent with fatigue and thirst. One of our scouts joined us shortly after, with the intelligence of a few gallons of stagnated water, about three miles off; but though entirely out, and suffering extremely for the want of it, we pushed on. The weather, which had been for four days past rigorously cold, suddenly changed about and became oppressively warm. Late in the day, we fell in with a trail at the foot of the mountains going north, and followed it until night. It proved to be a timber trail, and keeping it through a valley for fourteen miles, it brought us to thickets of dwarfish pine, much of which was cut and taken away, evidencing, to our surprise, we were at no great distance from settlements. We again spent the night without water, though we had examined every fissure and hollow for it we could discover along the way. Our thirst was becoming too intolerable for sleep, and we left camp with the first rays of returning light. A short distance in advance, we found a few isolated clumps of palmetto, whose bitter and nauseous wood we chewed, and thus in some degree moistened our swollen tongues and parching lips. The valley over which we were passing became narrower as we proceeded, until it sunk into a ravine, penetrating between two lofty mountains. Along its gloomy bed we now dragged our failing limbs, glaring anxiously around and above at every step, for some sign of moisture, and halting at short intervals, to listen for the heavenly music of a water-brook. It was vain to look, or listen. Several of the more tired of our party began this evening to fling away their muskets and haversacks: becoming too weak for the first, and the little remnant of food contained in the latter growing too dry to be forced down their husky throats.

Short and few were the words interchanged amongst us. The battalion, broken into squads of seven and ten, scattered at irregular distances, sullenly followed our athletic leader and his more robust associates, reckless of where, or in what direction they were proceeding. When darkness fell around us, little heed was taken of where we should bivouac, stopping mechanically at the first spot whose area of level surface offered us room to lie down on. Sentries had ceased to be set, messes were broken up; officers no longer aspired to command, or soldiers deigned a show of obedience. Worn out with the march, each man dropped to sleep where he halted, scornful of fire, food, or security from the foe; and forgetful of home, freedom, every thing, so he might steep his wandering senses in oblivion, and quell the fiery pangs that racked him. Many slept, but more babbled through the long chilly night, of forgotten springs and streams, whose mocking mirage, flaring fancies conjured up in dreams.

Another morning found us sluggishly crawling towards the top of a higher mountain than any we had yet encountered, buoyed with the hope of discovering from its summit some landmark that might reveal us water. After hours of toil and labour, we gained the ascent, where murmurs of reviving animation stole out from lips hitherto sealed with despair. A wide and partially wooded expanse of valley, spread out underneath the eye, indicating to those best skilled in such evidences, the certain existence of the all-engrossing object. Pausing to rest, whilst all eyes were busy in searching out the most promising localities in which to prosecute a discovery, we at length began our descent, in various detachments, down the rugged and lengthening sides of the mountain.

It was full noon before the foremost of our men reached the bottom, where, having arrived, they dispersed them in still smaller squads through the plain, each man intent upon his own relief, and indifferent to every sentiment or circumstance beside. The largest body, led by Cameron, kept their course northwest, whilst the rest, without guides, and regardless of destination, sallied off towards every point of the compass. In the extremity of our suffering, the enemy were entirely forgotten; or if thought of at all, longed for as friends who would bring us relief, rather than as enemies from whom we had any thing to dread or endure. Had the valley that enclosed us been filled with furious wild beasts, they would scarce have obstructed the hunt we were then making for water. The evening wore off again, without a solitary signal-smoke being visible in any direction, to tell that our friends had discovered the desired relief. Scattered at unknown distances from each other, we spent another terrible night of lunacy and torture. Not a track or mark showed that the solitude over which we rambled had ever before been visited by walking, creeping, or winged things.

Six days of unintermitted and fiery toil through these arid and rugged wastes had elapsed, since the thirsting lips of any had been moistened with a drop of water. The sufferings of this seventh day, as recounted by our men after they were once more united, beggar all powers of description. Those slept who could; and others (unsettled in mind), wandered off they knew not where; until picked up by the enemy's cavalry, they were restored to consciousness by stinted draughts of water, and led or carried to camp. Disbanded and dispersed, no resistance was any where offered to the foe, nor is it believed that if embodied, our united force, emasculated in spirit, and emaciated in body as they were, could have successfully opposed one-half their numbers. Victory, too, when obtained, had no allurements to tempt, save one barbarous and savage mitigation of our pangs, too horrid to recite.

Cameron, with about seventy of our skeleton corps, were allured into camp at night by the smoke from the Mexican fires, erroneously supposing them the concerted signals of friends. They arrived within the ambuscade late at night, staggering with weakness, and being promptly surrounded by superior numbers of the enemy, were disarmed and bound on the instant. Tied in pairs, as fast as they were brought in, they lay grouped about within the lines, raving, begging, and menacing the Mexican soldiery for water. Of this our captors had but a limited supply themselves, having brought with them only what their gourds contained, and being forbidden by their officers to administer it in any but the most sparing quantities.

We set off at dawn for the Pass Benado, some twelve miles distant, where the main body of the Mexican force engaged in pursuit of us, were encamped. Most of our men were compelled to ride, and those on foot so feeble as to walk with difficulty and require frequent halts. Out of one hundred and eighty who had descended into the valley, about a hundred had been taken, and a large body of the enemy's cavalry were still behind in quest of the remainder.

When we arrived late in the evening at Pass Benado, where the enemy's infantry were stationed, our wasted and attenuated forms struck horror and compassion into the minds of all who saw us. No congregation of the newly-risen dead, who had been buried in the ragged cerements of the pest-house, could have inspired such mingled emotions of surprise and disgust, as did our ghastly and tattered crew. All half naked—some barefooted, and others with an odd shoe and sandal—legs torn and lacerated by rocks and brambles—our hair and beards matted and bushy, shading profiles cut down by hunger and suffering to the pallid, pinched, and sharpened expression of death–eyes sunk into the very beds of their sockets, and sparkling with fitful light, half frenzied, half ferocious, inspired doubts with the beholder whether we came from the asylum or the churchyard.

Thirty-four more of our unfortunate fellows joined us that night at Benado. As soon as taken, they were all searched, robbed, bound, and brought to camp. Steeled against every indignity, and totally reckless of the future, their constant, increasing, *stereotyped* prayer was for water. The names of our officers, from the leader down to the corporals, were carefully noted down, and the victims removed to a separate camp, where they were allowed no communication whatever with the men. Bound with raw-hide tugs, two and two, they were strictly watched through the day, and made at night to lie down in rows, with a strong patrol over them, to see they did not rise under any pretext. Cameron was separately guarded, with his hands securely pinioned behind his back.

On the 25th, we commenced our march, tied in pairs and halting at every watering-place we passed. This nectarine beverage was now supplied us in greater quantities, and who amongst us that partook of its gradually augmenting doses can ever forget the ecstacy with which he quaffed it. We also began to swallow small morsels of food, which were offered in much greater quantities than we either relished or could consume.

At nearly every ranch where we stopped, straggling parties of our unfortunate friends were brought up, bound and guarded with a vigilance wholly thrown away, as none seemed to cherish a solitary sigh for deliverance. From these we obtained intelligence of several of our companions who had perished in the mountains. During every day's march, our list of sick was increased, until near a third of our numbers were mounted, and such as continued on foot were so weak as required the most moderate stages to enable them to get on at all.

Still the apprehensions of our guard seemed to increase, far outstripping our improving strength, till at the ranch San Antonio we underwent the solemn farce of having our raw-hide thongs replaced by heavy iron handcuffs, used in binding their malefactors, when transported from place to place. Unaccustomed as we were to smile at any thing, (but the appearance of food and water,) we could not repress a general laugh at this gratuitous precaution on the part of our gaolers.

It was not until the 1st of March that we arrived in the suburbs of Saltillio; where, having halted, we were detained several hours under the alleged plea that our commander (General Mexier) was behind, and we were awaiting his coming up before entering the town.

This commandant, uniting in his person the offices of Governor of the State of Coahuila and general, had that morning received a despatch from Santa Anna, directing him to butcher us all if recaptured; which he nobly resolved to disobey, and for which he was shortly afterwards removed from his civil employment. The struggle between his obedience and humanity resulted in our being marched into town, amidst the greatest rejoicing, and relocked in our ancient quarters.

Chapter X

*Error in leaving the road explained ·
Cameron · Troops by whom we were
recaptured · Arrival of our men from the
Mountains · Visit from American Wagoners ·
Their deportment and communications to us · Five of
our sick Baptized · Examination of our Interpreters ·
Colonel Baragan · Arrival of Guard from San
Luis · Leave Saltillio · Reach the Salado ·
Order from the Government · Draw for
our Lives · Seventeen of our Comrades
Executed · Their Names · Escape
of Shepherd.*

Returning from the Pass de Benado to the Ranch San Antonio, we were fully able to appreciate the fatal blunder we had committed in turning off from the Monclova road at this ranch, and entering the mountains. From the point beyond the San Antonio at which we left the road to Pass Benado is sixty miles, not much more than a good day's journey in the plight in which we then were. Our circuit through the mountains, which brought us within fifteen miles of the pass, occupied us nine days; and the Mexican force sent in pursuit of us only reached the pass the day before they captured us. By keeping the road, therefore, we should have been more than a week in advance of them, had plenty of forage for our horses, and provisions and water for ourselves. No force was on our direct line of route to resist us, nor could any from the towns south of us have gained such certain intelligence of our direction as to have intercepted our passage to the Rio Grande. We should have had it in our power, on nearing the Texan frontier, to have mounted every man of the party; and the farmers all dreaded us too much not to facilitate our escape, in lieu of rendering any efficient aid in our recapture.

The unfortunate Cameron is in no degree responsible for the error, having repeatedly declared his intention of going to the left of Monclova, and being overruled in his purpose of keeping the road by the influence of a majority of the captains, backed by the dogged resolution of many of their men. It was fated we should be thus devoted, and as heaven willed, it occurred.

The troops employed in retaking us were estimated at fifteen hundred men, being nothing more than militia or minute men, or, as they termed themselves, *procidialos*. Each of these men was armed with a hanger, carbine, and lance, and uniformed in leather jerkins and open pants, with low-crowned wool-hats, ornamented with white bands. An enormous guard of this scum kept strict watch over our prison, until a regular force could be obtained from San Luis Potosi, to escort us that far on our way to the capital. We had also to await the further pleasure of Santa Anna, in regard to our disposal, his very benevolent design of a general extermination having been thwarted by the generosity of Mexier, as before related.

Other small parties of our men continued to arrive from the mountains from day to day, sometimes brought in by couples, and at other times in greater numbers.

On the 9th, Barney Bryant, a prisoner, died, but none of us were permitted to witness his interment.

Several American wagoners of Zacatecas called to see us on the 12th, who informed us, with less sensibility than they would probably have displayed in recounting the loss of a horse, that an order had arrived directing every tenth man of us to be shot. The brutes seemed to consider it a precious privilege to be first to communicate the tidings, thinking, no doubt, it would prove a decided mitigation of the blow to have it come from Anglo-Saxon lips; and ciphering out the exact amount of the propitiatory sacrifice, they indulged in a few strictures upon our folly in being recaptured, and went away. Of course we put no faith in their assertions, as it was uncorroborated by the guard, who were ever too delighted in harassing us to omit such an opportunity, had it been true.

Five of our sick were baptized by a Catholic priest, and united to the church of Rome. There was no apostasy in the case, none of them being previously of any faith at all, and all standing in most especial need of some form of sanctification. Broken in health, and dejected with their lot, they sought consolation from above against their earthly woes, and appealed on high for support and strength against sufferings too great for their physical fortitude. Their conversion, whether real or pretended, provoked sneers and taunts from their comrades, some of whom could not be brought to regard it in any light but a weak attempt to conciliate the Mexicans. If so intended, the *ruse* was unavailing, as, so far as could be discovered, it produced no amelioration of the hardships of their condition.

On the 19th inst., three of our men, who spoke the language most correctly, and ordinarily acted as interpreters, A. S. Thurman, W. Moore, and John Brennan, were taken from prison, and examined under oath with the most rigid strictness, touching all the circumstances connected with our charge upon the guard. This evidence was intended for a court-martial, which had been ordered for the trial of Colonel Baragan, who, we afterwards learned, was broke, the accusation against him involving not only a charge of carelessness, but actual connivance in our escape. Of the truth of the first, we will not pretend to determine; but of the latter, there was not only no foundation whatever in fact, but not the remotest ground for suspicion. Had Baragan's men been true to him, but few of us would have survived the conflict; whilst double the number of his guard would not have deterred our attempt, nor repelled our attack, had they reflected the cowardice of those whom we did disperse. Baragan's soldiership was too mixed up with the elements of honour and humanity to find favour with the cowardly butcher whom he served; and, in removing him from the service, Santa Anna and the vile agents of his work, got rid of an eloquent reproach upon their own cruelty and pusillanimity.

The escort from Potosi having arrived at Saltillio on the 21st instant, we took up the line of march on the next morning, strongly handcuffed in pairs. Our new guard consisted of two full companies of cavalry, and one of infantry; the whole commanded by Colonel Ortis, particularly distinguished for his courage, and also esteemed (outside his profession) a man of generosity and benevolence.

Our route was over the identical road, from Saltillio to the Ranch Salado, heretofore described. Three days' severe marching brought us to St. Salvador, and the fourth day, (Friday the 25th of March,) after a journey of twenty miles, we reached the Ranch Salado, about three o'clock in the afternoon. This dismal farm-house, so late the scene of our triumphant emancipation, was now destined to become the theatre of one of the most cowardly and brutal murders ever enacted within the precincts of the robber-haunted region that surrounds it.

Chapter X

Jaded with the barbarous stages imposed on us in our fettered condition, and worn down with the severity of our morning's tramp, we entered our former quarters (the coural of the ranch), and gladly sought repose for our wearied limbs upon the filthy floor of the shed that ran round the enclosure. The morning had been clear and beautiful, and the noon warm to sultriness; but a few miles before we reached the ranch the sky became suddenly overcast, and fierce gusts of wind came whistling along the plain, blinding us with clouds of sand, and whirling the heavy leathern caps of the cavalry from their heads as lightly as though they were children's bonnets. So sudden and violent a transition of the element around us would have passed unheeded at any other time or place. But occurring on the eve of our return to a spot with which we were connected by memories of blood and violence, whose transactions vague rumour had also associated with some impending atonement, inspired a presentiment of approaching evil in the minds of most of us. Still there was nothing either in the communications or deportment of our guard along the road, to excite the slightest suspicion of their design, and by the time we had reached our pen and huddled under its shelter, the tempest began to lull and our apprehensions were departed.

But a few minutes had elapsed before a group of Mexican officers entered our quarters, and one of them, holding a paper in his hand, directed the interpreter to summon us around him, when he proceeded to read its contents in Spanish to the assembled prisoners. As no second order enforcing the execution of the one from Santa Anna commanding our deaths had been received at Saltillio, a hope had sprung up amongst many, that some possible clemency might be in store for them. A few, therefore, of the more sanguine, pushed their way into the circle, and bent their eager eyes on the reader, half expecting his communication to be a mandate for our release.

Who can describe the thrill of horror and consternation that electrified every heart, when the interpreter, in broken and tremulous tones, announced it as an order from the supreme government, directing every tenth man amongst us to be shot! the lots to be decided on the instant, and the execution to follow immediately. So entirely unexpected was this murderous announcement, so atrocious in its character, and so inhuman and indecent in the haste of its consummation, that a stupor seemed to pervade the whole assembly, not a word escaping from the lips of any for more than a minute. The silence was at length interrupted by the interpreter, who, in obedience to his directions, proceeded to inform us further, that *all* had been sentenced to the same fate, but the *humane* government had been graciously pleased to commute the just claim to this decimal exaction.

A low clatter of the handcuffs was now heard, as some of the most desperate of our fellows essayed to free themselves from their shackles. This had been foreseen and provided against. An order was promptly given us to fall back within the shed, and the doorway and top of the sunken wall bristled with the muzzles of muskets presented to enforce it. We were helpless as the bound victim under the sacrificial knife, and had no alternative but to obey. Whilst we were marshalled in an extended file, a Mexican subaltern and soldier entered the yard together, bearing a bench and earthen crock. The bench was placed before the officer who had communicated the order, and the crock set upon it, containing one hundred and seventy-four beans, (the number of prisoners present,) amongst which were *seventeen black ones*. A handkerchief, so folded as to hide the colour of the beans, was then thrown over the crock, and a list of our names, taken down when we were recaptured, placed in the hands of the interpreter. When these funeral preliminaries were completed, the name of our dauntless leader was first called, who, with a step as stately and brow as serene as he ever previously wore, stepped forward and drew. Each name continued to be called in their order on the list, and the individual compelled to draw, until the seventeen black beans were taken from the crock. When a bean was drawn, it was handed to the officer, and the bowl well shaken before the lottery proceeded. As they drew, each person's name was entered upon another memorandum, with the colour of his bean. In many instances the doomed victim was enforced to revisit the fatal urn, to allow the comrade to whom he was chained to try the issues of life and death.

Appalling as was the first effect of the order, and rapidly and voraciously as our self-dug graves yawned around, not a step faltered, nor a nerve shook, as the sickening ceremonial proceeded. Several of the Mexican officers seemed deeply affected, shedding tears profusely, and turning their backs upon the murderous spectacle. Others again leaned forward over the crock, to catch a first glimpse of the decree it uttered, as though they had heavy wagers upon the result.

Three-fourths of the beans were exhausted before the fatal seventeen were drawn. When the sacrifice was made up, the victims' names were called over, their persons scrutinized, and being removed outside, their irons were knocked off. A few of us were permitted to go out and take a hasty leave of them. A priest had accompanied the march from Saltillio, who was now present to offer them extreme absolution; but only two could be prevailed on to accept of his intercession. Major Robert Dunham, being importuned to confess him to the holy father, repelled the proposition with warmth, preferring, like a good Protestant, to shrive himself, which he knelt down and did mutely and earnestly. This brave and honest man was then solicited by the rest to offer up a prayer in their behalf; but, as he was about to comply, he was rudely stopped by the officer on duty, who sternly and profanely forbade it. As the hour of twilight advanced, two files of infantry, consisting of twenty men each, with the whole of the cavalry, escorted the doomed party to the eastern wall, selected as the site of their execution. Here, being made to kneel down, with their faces to their butchers, they were blindfolded and shot, in two parties, successively, nine first, and eight soon afterwards.

Huddled together in the stalls of the coural, the surviving prisoners were forced to sit down, and a heavy body of sentinels placed over us, with their firelocks cocked and at a present, ordered to shoot the first man who should move or speak whilst the execution was progressing.

Tears forced their way down many a rugged cheek, as, silent and manacled, we listened to the mournful and plaintive notes of the dead march, swelling and sinking on the ear, as the procession rounded our prison, to the eastern flank of the ranch. The wall against which the condemned were placed, was so near us we could distinctly hear every order given, in halting and arranging the command for the work of death. The murmured prayers of the kneeling men, stole faintly over to us—then came the silence that succeeded, more eloquent than sound—then the signal taps of the drum—the rattle of the muskets, as they were brought to an aim—the sharp burst of the discharge, mingled with the shrill cries of anguish and heavy groans of the dying, as soul and body took their sudden and bloody leave.

The names of the victims of this perfidious and most atrocious tragedy, were—Thomas L. Jones, James M. Ogden, John S. Cash, Pat-

94

rick Maher, Henry Whaling, Major Robert Dunham, William Rowan, Major J. D. Cocke, Robert Harris, James Torrey, J. M. Thompson, C. M. Roberts, James Turnbull, E. E. Esta, Captain William M. Eastland, M. C. Wing, and James L. Shepherd.

In counting the corpses the ensuing morning, the body of the latter could not be found, and various were the strange surmises indulged by the Mexicans and recounted to us in explanation of its absence. Dead or alive, the vanished priest had the credit of having carried him off; for what use, none who asserted it undertook to conjecture. Certain it was he was missing, and his mysterious disappearance continued unexplained to any of us for months afterwards. Captain C. Buster and one of his men (Toops) having been left in the mountains, managed to elude the Mexican cavalry, and succeeded in reaching the banks of the Rio Grande, on their way to Texas. Here, after all their toils and hardships, their good fortune deserted them; and, being recaptured by the enemy, they were brought to Saltillio, where in prison they learned from their gaolers the sad particulars of poor Shepherd's fate.

When kneeling with his unfortunate companions, they received the fire of their executioners, all were killed or mortally wounded, save Shepherd. The ball aimed at his head passed along his cheek, cutting his face severely, but inflicting nothing more than a bad flesh-wound. At the discharge, he fell with the rest of his companions forward on his face, and bleeding profusely affected to be dead. Here he lay, without motion or apparent animation, until the soldiers retired, and, night coming on, immediately escaped to the mountains. Secreting himself by day, and travelling by night, for several weeks, ignorant of the way, and restrained by apprehensions of exposure from inquiring, he was at length compelled, by hunger, thirst, and debility, to surrender himself; and, being carried to Saltillio and recognised by his former executioners, was led directly to the public square and shot to death, amidst the pitiless exultations of its citizens.

Chapter XI

A glance at our murdered companions ·
The Hacienda St. John · Baptism of more of
our men · Their Catholicism · Beauty of the
village Benado · Colonel Ortis · San Luis Potosi ·
Death of five more of our men · Freed from our
hand-cuffs · Mexican Felons and Soldiers ·
San Felipe De Lazos · Paintings · San
Miguel · Mine of Valenciana · Plain
of Baxio · Marquis of Joral.

The next morning as we left the shambles of the Salado, we caught a mournful glance of the mangled bodies of our comrades. Their stiffened and unsepulchred bodies, weltering in blood, lay where they had fallen; whilst their rigid countenances, pallid and distorted with agony, appealed in death for retribution on their slayers. And many were the vows of vengeance registered that moment against their cowardly assassins; and fearfully will they yet be redeemed, when the hour of atonement rolls round. At the ranch we parted company with the infantry, who returned to Saltillio; the infamous miscreants having only been brought thus far to perform the butchers' work agreed upon. These were the identical heroes whom, with naked hands, we had disarmed and routed the morning of our break at this place, and who, smarting under a sense of their disgrace, had petitioned for the brutal employment just despatched. Should a Texan army ever penetrate to Saltillio, let the memory of this transaction claim the amplest expiation.

After a march of forty-two miles, we reached an enormous hacienda on Sunday evening, called the St. John, equal in the extent of its buildings and the area it embraces, to many of the lesser villages of Mexico. The territory attached to it, and under cultivation, seemed sufficient to require the labour of a thousand hands, and its yield of a single year more than adequate to the wishes of ordinary cupidity.

Our quarters for the night were unusually comfortable, and our rations sumptuous in comparison with the customary fare allotted us. In the morning, after being paraded for the march, we were kept waiting for near three hours until the ceremony of baptism was performed upon four other of our men. The dissemination of Catholicism amongst our fellows seemed the more difficult to account for on any rational grounds, as not a soul of them had heard but a solitary mass in the country, and not a word of that intelligible to more than three out of the entire number. The converts, however, seemed extremely sanctimonious and devout after the ceremony, preserving as profound a silence, touching the mysteries of their new faith, as entered apprentices of Masonry.

His reverence the padre was allowed but little time to enlighten them in the doctrines of his venerable creed, and most probably their imperfect acquaintance with them, sealed their lips in decorous taciturnity.

Our route continued to the southward, travelling from twenty to thirty miles a day, and passing on the way many large and well-built ranches, surrounded by fertile plantations of cotton, maguey, corn, and wheat, that gave an aspect of plenty and opulence to the country. At one of these farms at which we stopped for the night, called La Guna, (owned or managed by a Frenchman) a prisoner, (S. M'Clellan), died of pleurisy. The succeeding day (the 31st of March), we entered the village Benado, where we were received with becoming humanity, and lodged in commodious and agreeable quarters.

Here our commander, Colonel Ortis, had promised us we should rest a day, in virtue of which we had borne without repining several previous long and irksome marches. We arrived early in the afternoon of Saturday, and after enjoying the refreshment of a good and substantial dinner, were conducted by the guard to the nearest suburbs, where, in a beautiful stream that bisects the town, we were allowed the luxury of a bath. As far as the eye could reach, above and below the village, the banks of the little rivulet were enamelled with gardens and orchards, robed in bloom, and breathing the fragrance of every fruit and flower, that meet in emulous rivalry from north and south, on this edge of the tropics.

Whilst some of these trees, had barely opened their young and aromatic blossoms, the boughs of others were loaded with ripened and luscious harvests, that glittered in hues of gold and purple, as they basked them in the radiance of an April sun. The coffee and nopal tree mingled their contrasted foliage in avenues between, and thickets of roses, of every dye and perfume, wept on the bosom, or smiled over the surface, of the liquid mirror below. It was an evening of sunshine, love, and beauty. From behind a little promontory, scarce a pistol-shot from where we bathed, pavilioned to the very lip of the wave with densest foliage, came the bird-voices of joyous girls, disporting their Naiad forms in the cool element, whilst clusters of children from the opposing bank, re-echoed their mirthful shouts and pantomimed their antics with gleesome mimicry. Flame-feathered birds, and velvet butterflies, darted from spray to spray midst the shrubbery, and choirs of exulting insects floated through the scented air, or hymned their tiny strains from leaf and flower. The magic of a golden sunset flung its splendour over all, as we resumed our chains and vestments, and filed off towards the prison.

Colonel Ortis, though a rigid martinet, and inflexible in all that appertained to the interests of the service, manifested the greatest kindness and benevolence to us, in every thing that he considered compatible with his duties. Whilst on the march, we had occasion to remark the delicacy of his humanity, in guarding us from every insult from the people or the soldiers, refraining from all painful exhibitions of us in the towns and haciendas through which we passed, and enforcing the most comfortable quarters and rations to be procured, wherever we stopped. Instead of surrounding us with his cavalry upon the road, subjecting us to the intolerable annoyance of the dust which they raised, he disposed them invariably in our rear, preferring himself and the guard should be incommoded, sooner than add unnecessarily to our inconveniences. Our sick were also carefully provided for, riding on the way, and furnished with every practicable comfort when arrived at quarters. It is true, to be sure, the distances heretofore assigned us to accomplish in a single march, (ironed as we were,) seemed unreasonable; but they were usual for the Mexican infantry, and appeared in his eyes but pleasant promenades to Texan endurance and hardihood. In executing the bloody edict of Santa Anna at the Salado, he but acted in obedience to the mandate of his superiors, and palliated his unavoidable agency in the ruthless deed, by withholding his presence from any part of the spectacle. He was a Biscayan by descent, and ranked high in his profession for courage and accomplishments.

Four days of moderate marching brought us, through a rich and populous region, to the renowned city of San Luis Potosi, the capital

of the state and intendancy of that name. This city, the largest we
had yet encountered in Mexico, stands in a plain of luxuriant herbage, interspersed with fields and gardens, over which the cupolas
and tapering spires of its numerous churches are visible for a great
distance. The town itself was formerly noted for the beauty and dur-
ability of its buildings, though age and the decline of its wealth and
trade have made serious alterations in its ancient splendour. Its convents and cathedrals, barracks, prisons, mint, and governor's palace,
exhibit a painful contrast in their massive and still elegant exteriors,
with the low and dusky houses of the suburbs, built of unbaked
brick, and covered with soiled and dirty cement. Both together have
been computed to contain a population of seventy thousand souls,
which though reduced, may still be estimated at near fifty thousand.

The inhabitants of this city and state enjoy a better reputation for
industry and manufacturing enterprise, than most of their countrymen, and supply the states of Zacatecas, Leon, Coahuila, and Duran-
go, with clothing, hats, shoes, and other productions of their skill.
Its silver mines of Catorce, Guadalcazar, and Charcas, are amongst
the richest in Mexico: the former surpassing in the purity and abundance of its ore, any mines of the republic, except those of Guana-
huata.

The prison in which we were lodged, was an unfinished room of the hospital, one hundred feet in length, and near thirty in breadth. Here we were freed from our handcuffs, which we had worn for more than a month, and supplied with a plenty and good quality of food, whose excellence and abundance were more eloquent than volumes, in praise of the famous markets of San Luis. Our sick were likewise provided with places in the hospital, where, notwithstanding they received the best attention and nursing it afforded, five of them died after arriving. Their names were Beard, Caufman, Rockfeller, Halderman, and Hill. Four of our men whom we left at the Salado, were also found here in the hospital.

We left San Luis on the 10th inst., with an accession to our captive numbers of near three hundred convicts, condemned for various offences by their laws to serve in the army, for periods graduated to the enormity of their crimes. The Mexicans have neither galleys nor penitentiaries in which to confine and punish their felons; so that whenever the crime of the transgressor falls below capital punishment, he is condemned to the disgrace and peril of that service, which is every where else esteemed an honour and privilege to embrace. To the Mexican felon it is an ignominy and a dread; the uniform of his country a badge of his past turpitude; and the support of its renown, and defence of its soil and rights, a compulsory and loathsome task. Of such material is one half of its regular soldiery composed, and here is a key at once to their shameful cowardice, and brutal instincts. Their pay is nominally twelve dollars per month, exclusive of rations, uniform, and equipments. But only a fraction of this is paid them, the balance being commuted or withheld; leaving the government at no greater cost for their maintenance than would be required for their support in jail. Such sentiments as a love of glory, or sense of honour, amongst them, is seldom or never found, being animated by no stronger attachment to their service than the opportunity it affords them to pillage and thieve with impunity. Many of their lieutenants are younger than the youngest cadet at West Point; and captains and colonels may be found still in their minority.

The best of their troops, and the balance of their army, are recruited in a manner as little creditable to the national justice, as these general jail deliveries are to the national defence.

A sergeant, with a band of trusty fellows, goes into the fields or Indian villages, and selecting the youngest and ablest-bodied labourers, commands them by the authority with which he is empowered, to follow him. If they obey, so much the better, but if they resist or attempt to escape, they are lassoed on the spot, bound in pairs, and marched off without further ceremony to the nearest barracks. After being drilled until they acquire a knowledge of the manual and ordinary routine of duty, they are uniformed, and enticed by trifling bounties to enlist for various terms of service, from two to ten and fifteen years. Against such impressment there is no appeal; desertion in time of peace being punished with cruel floggings, and in time of war, invariably with death.

This rascally addition to our force, and the removal of our irons, induced the augmentation of our guard by a strong body of infantry; and they, with our previous escort, the cavalry, continued under the command of Colonel Ortis, who accompanied us at the special solicitation of our officers, deputed to act in all matters of general interest for the prisoners.

We continued south through cultivated and beautiful districts, marching sometimes twenty, and at others thirty miles a day, and stopping for the night alternately at large haciendas, or in villages and towns. When informed of the population of many of these groups of hovels we passed, it was impossible to credit the amount of souls ascribed to them, unless we had personally seen the swarms they poured out, to reciprocate our inspection. Each kennel seemed to contain a score of inmates, and each larger building its scores.

In approaching San Felipe, said to contain fifteen thousand inhabitants, the extensive level plains over which we journeyed were being watered from numerous wells sunk in the fields; the water drawn up by the labourers with sweeps, and scattered over the surface by means of troughs.

At De Lazos, a beautiful and well-built village, with a church in the square whose architecture would adorn the largest city, we were quartered in a meson, or hotel, containing numerous paintings illustrative of Mexican history, and some of them very creditable productions of art. They were represented as the achievements of a young Italian, who flying the country to escape punishment for some crime, left them to the confiscation that chance might devote them to. The violation of law must have been a most heinous one, to have induced his precipitate and desperate abandonment of a people his brush had so unscrupulously flattered.

On the 16th, we reached San Miguel, one of the most picturesque towns of Guanaxuato, the smallest, but the most densely populated of the Mexican states. The great mammoth silver mine of this state, Valenciana, is reported to have yielded in thirty-seven years 165,000,000 of dollars. For many years its produce has considerably declined, the revolution and subsequent disorders of the country having interrupted its operations to such a degree as to require enormous expenditures for drainage and repairs of the works.

San Miguel is the most southeastern of a number of villages that stud the plain of Baxio, a fertile and productive table-land, celebrated as the site on which were enacted some of the most memorable tragedies of the revolution. It has several manufactories of cotton and wool, amongst the latter of which are made the finest and most ornamental blankets worn by the Mexicans.

In the northwestern part of Guanaxuato lie the hereditary possessions of the opulent house of Joral. The lordly proprietor of these princely domains was supposed able, at the breaking out of the revolution, to mount fifty thousand cavalry from the herds of horses that roamed his extensive pastures, and support them without difficulty for a twelvemonth with the marketable stock from his countless droves of cattle. His connected domain was reputed to embrace ten thousand square miles, and his shepherds, herdsmen, husbandmen, and tenantry, to reach to twice that number of persons.

Chapter XII

Deserted Monastery · Queretaro · Convent
of Santa Clara · Aqueduct · Major Murray ·
Tula · Reverence of Convicts for Religious Houses ·
Wetoke · Strange Coincidences · Captain Cameron ·
His Execution and Character · Arrival at Santiago ·
View of Mexico · Visit from Foreigners ·
Proposition from Governor · Indignation
of Prisoners · American Minister · His
advice adopted · New Uniforms.

Twenty-eight miles from San Miguel, we quartered at night in the chapel of a deserted monastery. Though long unused, it was but little dilapidated, bearing none of those evidences of wanton violence that mark the desecration of these monastic asylums in other lands, where war or civil strife have expelled their inmates. How various or how unholy soever had been its occupants, since the removal of the saintly brotherhood, a reverential regard for its ancient usages seemed to have preserved even the most fragile portions of the building from all destruction but that which time and neglect had wrought.

An easy march on the following day brought us to Queretaro, the capital of the little state of that name, west of Vera Cruz, and one hundred and twenty-five miles from the point of our destination. This city is nearly, if not quite, as large as San Luis Potosi, more beautiful in its site, and far more modern and chaste in the style of its construction. The houses are elegantly and commodiously built, and the streets, wide, with good side-walks, intersect each other at right angles, terminating in the three largest and principal squares of the town. The magnificence of its churches and convents excite universal admiration, the largest of the latter (Santa Clara) being said to embrace an area of twelve thousand feet in circumference. But its most imposing feature is its ten miles length of aqueduct, whose massive and lofty arches, built of enormous blocks of stone, transported from a distance, must have cost millions of treasure to erect.

At San Juan, a small village beyond, Major Murray joined us, having been left here sick in the hospital; and we in turn left a man (Martin) extremely ill, who died shortly after our departure. Fifty miles farther on we rested at Tula, a diminutive village, situated in a low flat valley, where we met and were delivered over to the guard despatched to escort us to Mexico. Here we were quartered in consecrated lodgings again, occupying the upper portico of an old church, whilst our comrades, the convicts, appropriated the lower one. These fellows, many of them of the most sinister and desperate expression of countenance, trained to plunder and assassination from infancy, and who would pillage a shrine, when at large, as unscrupulously as they would a shop, seemed struck with a solemn and dreadful remorse for their sins, whenever brought within the precincts of a building that had been dedicated to holy uses. Impenitent and jovial on the road, they cheered their confinement at hacienda, meson, or in prison, with songs and jests and games, but brought within the influence of stone and mortar sanctified by the exercises of religion, a superstitious awe seemed to possess their inmost souls, and aves and penitential prayers took the place of their reckless jollity. A mile from the church next morning, the spell was dissipated, and the redemptionless felons were themselves again.

Sunday, the 24th of April, we reached Huitoke, another inconsiderable village, where comfortable quarters and an ample supply of provisions were assigned us. As we approached this place in the evening, we endured a sudden caprice of the weather, followed by a storm of wind and rain, as instantaneous and furious as that which heralded our fatal return to the Salado. We may, therefore, be pardoned the weakness of noting them, in consideration of the extraordinary coincidences that succeeded their strange and unexpected occurrence. A month precisely had intervened since a similar explosion of the elements had knelled the bloody decimation of our little band; and the unsuspecting victim of another and as pitiless a murder, was now the first to confess his forebodings of impending doom.

The ill-starred Cameron, who had already shared the risks of the cruel and perilous lottery at the Salado, was awakened here at a late hour of the night from the pallet on which he slept, and being hurried half naked into a distant room, was unceremoniously informed he was to be shot next morning, without any explanation being assigned to him. His irons were replaced, and a strong guard set over him to intercept all communication with his comrades from without. The indignant murmurs of our men at this double perfidy and brutality, broke out next morning when paraded for the march, notwithstanding the gratuitous assurance from the Mexican officers that this was the last victim demanded. Desperate suggestions were whispered of a rescue; and the Mexican commander, apprehending the worst the dastardly deed deserved, pushed on with us, leaving Cameron in the hands of his assassins. The execution took place some hours after we left, nor were we ever able to learn any precise particulars of his death.

Thus perished, in the zenith of his manly vigour, Captain Ewen Cameron, a brave, noble and accomplished soldier and gentleman; as distinguished for all the virtues and humanities that adorn life, as he was the pride and idol of his comrades and acquaintances. A Scotchman by birth, and lineally descended from the warlike Highland clan whose name he bore, his magnanimous enterprise and sacrifices in the cause of freedom, will endear and preserve his memory as fondly amongst the gallant race from whom he sprung, as it will ever be cherished by that people in whose service he fell. Gentle, social, and loyal, he was the counterpart of that heroic Lochiel, whose romantic sensibility and generous devotion to the hapless house of Stuart, has been so faithfully and beautifully illustrated by the Wizard of Fiction and the Bard of Hope.

On Tuesday the 26th instant, just four months from the day on which we had surrendered at Mier, we entered the convent and prison of Santiago, situated near the northern environs of the Mexican capital. Tattered, squalid, and worn down by fatigue, sick at heart and despondent in hope, our sufferings and despair were alike forgotten, as we gazed with astonishment and admiration from out the valley we were traversing, upon this Rome of the new world, this model city of the universe. The domes and pinnacles of its churches, the turrets of its prisons and palaces—the massive walls of its convents and monastic edifices—draperied in the crimson hues of sunset, and mellowed by the purple shadows of the tall mountains around, gave it a look of dreamy enchantment, that filled us with emotions of joy and wonder. It was not until the portals of our prison had swallowed us up, man by man, that we ceased our fascinated inspection of the splendid panorama.

For near a week following our arrival at Santiago, great numbers of foreigners resident in the capital, come out to visit us. English, Germans, French, and Americans, seemed equally eager to hear the sad history of our disasters, and on their return to the city, transmitted us considerable supplies of clothing. Here we found the three boys whom Ampudia had detained in Matamoras, having cast them in prison there, upon intelligence of our break at the Salado, and shortly after sent them to Mexico. One of them, thirteen years old, (John Hill,) a brave and handsome little fellow, was afterwards liberated by Santa Anna, who has since charged himself with his education, and has him now at school in Mexico.

Through the partiality he is said to enjoy with the usurper, his brother and father (who likewise belonged to the expedition,) were successively released, and money provided them with which to reach home. He frequently visited us in our confinement, expressing the keenest solicitude for our welfare, and the most earnest hopes of our speedy deliverance. This was the boy whom the newspaper accounts of the battle of Mier represent to have killed *seventeen* Mexicans. He behaved with the gallantry of a veteran throughout that bloody fight, and we dare say, from the deliberation and the frequency of his shots, must have added largely to the enemy's loss. Here also we found a portion of our wounded, who had been left in Mier, and were no little amused at the many promotions they reported to have been bestowed on the Mexican officers engaged in that affair. These were doubtlessly contrived by the coxcombry of Ampudia, to swell to its greatest distention, the eclat of this, his first, last, and only triumph.

Lieutenant Crittenden, whom we had left amongst the sick at Matamoras, had been liberated before our arrival; and Mr. O. G. Phelps, (by whose father Santa Anna had been kindly treated in Texas,) was sent for and immediately presented with his freedom.

We were extremely well fed and cared for in this old convent, and rapidly recruiting our health and flesh under its humane discipline; when, some ten days after arriving, our agreeable respite was interrupted by a visit from the governor. This dignitary, Colonel ———, a morose, ill-favoured Cerberus, as ever turned bolt upon prisoner, came in and informed us, with an air and tone of the most touching philanthropy, he was having us all good comfortable clothes made. For these, when completed, so that we could make an unexceptionable appearance outside, his generous but indigent government expected we would perform some unspecified labour in return.

Beginning to fatten on the government larder, and our pride and spirits having revived with the general improvement of our habits, the proposition of the governor, notwithstanding it was couched in the most diplomatic terms, and delivered with insinuating address, was received with universal scorn and indignation. The interpreter was directed to inform this official of the supreme government, that the usages of all civilized and enlightened nations, ancient and modern, were strictly opposed to enforcing prisoners of war to any kind or degree of labour whatever; that the most solemn and exact guarantees against such degrading treatment had been demanded and given before our surrender; and that, sooner than submit to the imposition, we would prefer repeated decimations, until not enough of our band were left to cook the daily dinner allowed us.

This spirited protest, enforced by clenched fists and knit brows, was followed up by the unanimous passage of a resolution, declaratory of a determination neither to accept the clothes, nor engage in labour of any kind. The clothes were denounced as a specious bribe, by which to purchase our acquiescence in a gross infringement of the laws of civilized war; and both were sternly repudiated on the spot. The governor, mute with consternation at our ingratitude and injustice towards his benevolent but penniless government, departed and left us to the soothing influence of a night's reflection. After his retirement, the discussion continued, when it was discovered there was a strong clothes party sprung up amongst the more ragged of our fellows, who, however unanimous against the working proposition, were as unanimously inclined to spare the sensibilities of the government, and accept the vestments. By and by this faction increased, until a considerable majority appeared on ballot favourable to renewing the outward man, but as resolute as ever against the requirement to soil their new plumage with work.

Meanwhile the governor had communicated with his superiors in the city, and the affair getting wind, we were honoured next morning by a troop of friendly visiters, amongst whom came the American minister. Their united counsel to us was, to submit to the decision of the authorities, in both their propositions; and this advice they enforced with such a show of friendly and rational argument, as more than half reconciled us to their suggestions. They had barely retired, before our interpreter was summoned to the presence of the inflexible governor. Being shown the garments which were arrived, he was instructed to apprise us, that if we did not receive them willingly, they would be tried on us at the point of the bayonet. This was closing the door to all farther controversy, and we accordingly desired the wardrobe to be sent in.

And gay and jaunty uniforms they proved. To each man was presented a jacket and trousers of coarse flannel, with longitudinal stripes of alternate red and green, running up and down a ground of the same; a coarse domestic shirt with sandals to match, completed these *turnpike regimentals;* and roars of laughter and many a merry jest on government and each other, shook the old corridors of the prison as we accoutred us in the motley gear. When fully equipped, it would have puzzled Shakspeare's fantastic moralizer, the witty Lucio, to decide whether our dress bespoke the *foppery of freedom*, or the *morality of imprisonment*.

BOOK IV

Chapter XIII

*Leave Santiago for Tacubaya · Santa
Anna's country palace · His guards · Our
superintendent · Employment · Behaviour of the
men · Change of overseers · Stratagems to avoid work ·
Flogging prisoners · Change of superintendents ·
Visiters and equipages · Salute to Santa
Anna · His cowardice at Velasco.*

In our holiday suits we emerged next morning from the convent, and when paraded, received the arms selected us to wield in the service of the Mexican government. These consisted of wooden shovels of the rudest manufacture, crowbars, picks, and a coarse grass-sack each, capable of containing about fifty pounds, with rawhide straps at the mouth by which to carry them. Thus equipped, and escorted by a strong body of cavalry, we were taken through the suburbs of the city in a westerly direction; crowds of lazzaroni, and half-naked women and children, following and cheering us at every step. We were fettered before leaving the prison, two and two, our chains being about ten feet long, and weighing some twenty pounds. Each end of the chain was confined to the nearest ankle of the men, and suspended when walking from an iron hook, depending from a belt round the waist.

After zigzagging through byways and over highways for six miles through the valley, we reached the country palace of Santa Anna, at Tacubaya, destined as the scene of our future labours. This favourite residence of the Dictator is a large two-story stone edifice, built in the prevailing fashion of the country, and situated on a gentle eminence, above the village we have mentioned. It commands a most beautiful prospect of meadows, orchards, gardens, and shrubberies, in all directions around. A rough road of irregular descent leads from the palace to the town; and houses on either side the way, connected by extended stone walls, run up to the very foot of the ascent on

which the palace stands. A few miles farther west, rise the wooded and lofty mountains that circuit the valley; and dotting the plain, north, east, and south, are little hamlets and villas, chapels, mills, manufactories, and ruins, that lend the landscape the most exquisite features of the picturesque. Two full regiments of cavalry, and the same number of infantry, were quartered at short distances from each other in the plain below; whilst a life-guard of two companies are stationed in and about the palace, mounting guard over this republican president day and night.

On our arrival, a youthful cavalier, superbly mounted and uniformed, announced himself as Captain ——, who had been honoured with the appointment of superintending our operations. He spoke French as fluently as Spanish, and expressed himself in a mixed jargon of both languages, as desirous of treating us with the utmost humanity, and exacting as moderate a degree of labour from us as the exigencies of the public service would admit of. We were quite charmed with the very liberal and elevated sentiments of our superintendent, and assured him, in turn, of the personal happiness

it would afford us to do every thing in our power to carry out his magnanimous intentions respecting our comfort. In token of the very familiar footing upon which his frankness and generosity had placed us, various particular inquiries were addressed him in English, as to the health of his parents, and their consciousness of his whereabouts; and one more sportive gentleman of the chain-gang took the liberty to furtively assail his courser in the rear with a pebble, that caused him to rear and prance in the most entertaining manner. Whilst engaged in curbing his restive horse, many were the entreaties addressed him to trade, shovels, picks, and chains, being held up in the most tempting array, in offer for his horse.

Upon his retiring, we were trotted off to an old church, in the last stages of decay, one of its rooms having been fitted for our reception; but our guard, relishing these quarters as little as ourselves, prevailed on the superintendent to change them next day, and we were removed to a deserted powder-mill, much better adapted to our entertainment than the church. Here, after arranging our quarters and depositing our baggage, which consisted of old toggery smuggled from Santiago in the sacks, we were taken out to the road between the palace and town, whose grading and paving we were to be employed upon. Our good-natured overseer, to give us an overwhelming proof of his forgiveness and continued regard, selected our own officers as his deputies, and having explained the inclination of the grade, the width, and mode of construction to be observed in making the road, galloped away and left us alone to the task. Some twelve or fifteen of our more obliging comrades set to work in good earnest, digging and toiling as though they were to be rewarded for their drudgery by large shares of the stock, and have the management and control of the future pike in their own hands. The balance of us very coolly retired to the shelter of an umbrageous ash close by, under whose spreading foliage we spent the remainder of the day in inglorious repose. It was in vain our officers remonstrated, entreated, and reasoned, we continued our loll for weeks, sleeping and gossiping of home and friends, or engaged in elaborate and curious calculations of the enormous lapse of time required to finish the stupendous work assigned to us. When the superintendent in person denounced the slow progress of the road, an additional force was detailed from the voluptuous shades of the ash to forward the improvement, and the remainder, after several minutes' digging, retreated exhausted to their shelter again.

Of course this state of things was not expected to last always, nor did it. Our purpose was to resent the indignity aimed at us, by labouring as little and as profitlessly as we could possibly contrive, without coming to an open breach with our task-masters. Our convict garbs, our chains, and the vile toil to which we were daily driven, were appreciated in the light which they were intended, and most of us were determined to thwart the tyrant as far as we might, without incurring a discharge from the carbines of his guard. These last seemed to trouble themselves as little as practicable with us or our plans. They marched us to work in the morning, leaving a sentry or two to see we did not wander off, and retired to their parade-grounds; returned at noon and sunset for us, and being quartered in the rooms below, kept vigilant guard over our prison till the ensuing day. Our quarters were near a mile and a half from the place of labour, and as we breakfasted at six o'clock, returned to dinner at twelve, and supper again at five, it may be supposed little time was left to work, were we disposed so to appropriate it. Our fare here was as villanous as a parsimonious commissary and filthy cook could make it. In the morning, we received a pint of what the Mexicans called *atola*, which is nothing more than corn gruel, sweetened with a little sugar; at dinner we had a pint of soup, sometimes beans, and seven ounces of poor gluey beef, oftentimes spoiled, with a six ounce loaf of coarse brown bread. Our supper was a second and unimproved edition of breakfast.

Some weeks of this jovial life having elapsed, and but a few rods of the road completed, our officers were broke and degraded to the ranks, to make way for a set of ferocious brute convicts brought from Santiago. These were entrusted with our superintendence, and authorized to exact full labour of us. Armed with cudgels, and supported by a score of soldiers, they commenced business with a briskness that would have macadamized all Mexico in a twelve-month, could it have been kept up. Selecting one or two of the weaker men, by way of warning to the rest, they undertook to use their bludgeons on them, and were only prevented from crippling or murdering their victims by the joint interference of the soldiers and prisoners. Several of these rows came off, which had like to have proved serious, had not our defiant flourish of picks and stones intimidated soldiers and convicts alike from proceeding to extremities in their punishments. It was sufficiently demonstrated, however, that we could no longer repudiate our tasks with impunity, and we accordingly adopted a

change of tactics, yielding a seeming compliance with their demands, but in reality labouring no more, or effectively, than before.

The road was to be first graded, leaving it raised in the centre, and curbed on either edge. It was then to be covered with a layer of large pebbles, upon which was put one of finer, and the whole pounded hard with heavy mauls. These stones we were to pack from the bed of a little creek, about a mile distant, in the sacks we brought from the convent. All the time that could possibly be wasted, in going to or returning from the creek, was dissipated by slow walking, frequent rests, and the most deliberate filling of the bags that ever miser observed in putting away his hoards. After a sack was sufficiently filled to accommodate the load to the bearer's comfort, stumbles and falls were resorted to, to reduce the contents, until scarce ten pounds of the deposit arrived in safety. Holes were slit in the sacks, that freed the imprisoned pebbles at every step on the way; and brawny fellows, who never had an hour's sickness in their lives, would drop down in a fit, and require some ten of their comrades several hours to get them to quarters. About sixty men were employed on this branch of road-making, and their daily transportation of material did not amount at night to as much as a spavined pony could draw in a porter's hand-cart.

The digging department was very little, if any better carried on. Tools were hid, lost, broken, sold, or given away, every time the eyes of our overseers were off us, and nearly as much work destroyed as was finished. More than half our fellows were at one time in the hospital, some of them truly sick, but the most labouring under diseases so complicated as to defy the comprehension of any faculty on earth, and baffle every remedy prescribed them. At the end of two months, about one hundred yards of road were finished, and some patches of old pavement repaired, which should not have required the force employed above ten days at the farthest.

At the expiration of this time, Colonel ———, was directed by Santa Anna, to institute an examination into matters, and see if he could not fall upon some plan whereby to bring about an improvement. This officer affected the most profound indignation at the quality of the food which had been supplied us. He promptly suppressed the atola, substituting coffee twice a day in its stead, and furnished us farther with good fresh beef, allowing us Texan cooks in lieu of his dirty countrymen, who had heretofore prepared our meals. He moreover acquainted us, that he was confided by the president with every thing appertaining to our employment, government, and subsistence, and that whilst we should be scrupulously well-cared for in the future, he expected in return a greater amount of work.

This was a substantial change for the better, and all seemed more or less inclined to set-to and execute the task with becoming despatch. As a farther reward of diligence, the chains of the most faithful labourers were taken off, until, one by one, in three weeks' time, nearly the whole gang were relieved of their shackles. The work progressed with amazing rapidity, asses and carts being employed to transport the sand and gravel, instead of men. Colonel Rangel in the mean time presided over us with the most vigilant and exact justice. Whenever a prisoner was detected dodging his labour, he was immediately decorated with a pair of anklets and guard-chains, until, before the road was completed, many of the emancipated were rebound, preferring mild employment in irons, to more active labour without them.

This retreat of the Dictator was the frequent resort of the most opulent and distinguished families of the capital. Superb equipages were daily arriving and departing, of every style and model, from the quaint old Spanish coach, loaded with carving and gilding, and drawn by three spans of mules, bestridden by postilions, to the more chaste and elegant English carriage, plain in colour and construction, and with horses whose plight reflected the highest credit on granaries and grooms. Cavaliers splendidly mounted, with saddles and bridles richly embossed and ornamented, attired in open embroidered breeches of velvet or coloured leather, adorned with buttons, tassels, and lace; whilst over their roundabouts of fancy-coloured woollen or cotton cloth, were worn cloaks of velvet, often stiff with gold or silver.

Mexican love of pomp and splendour has but two mediums of external display, and these are in riding, and religious festivals. We seldom saw the Dictator, who kept himself entirely secluded from all but his visiters and guards, rarely going into the city, being content with airing himself on the terrace of his fortress. When he did pass us, it was in a great coach drawn by six mules, and surrounded by several hundred cavalry, without whom he never ventured out. On these occasions, we were duly apprised of his coming, and, being formed on each side of the way, by our punctilious superintendent, exchanged spade and pick-axe salutations with him, in return for an inclination from his presidential head. We were the more readily reconciled to this enforced courtesy towards him by the recollection of his own obsequiousness whilst a prisoner at Velasco, where, on coming ashore from the Invincible, such was his dread of popular frenzy, the coward took the Texan flag from the stern of the commodore's gig, and waved it to the Texans on the beach, in deprecation of their apprehended resentment.

Chapter XIV

Santa Anna's personal appearance ·
Sketch of his history · Passion for Cock-fighting.

Santa Anna's personal appearance is such as would command attention and scrutiny from the most careless observer at any time or place he might appear. His height is a little below six feet, and his proportions and bearing graceful and soldierly. His features are all those of a man of decided talent and character; mouth, eyes, brow, and nose, prominently expressive of the capacity of their possessor for the highest parts in any drama of life in which circumstances might cast him. In camp or field he is the imperious, unsympathizing embodiment of action and authority; in society and diplomacy he is represented as distinguished for the refinement and insinuation of his address. Though greatly surpassing any living Mexican in the leading qualities that constitute an able and successful commander, his personal intrepidity was ever questioned, and is now at a considerable discount. His exorbitant ambition and love of power would prefer the achievement of their arms through craft and fraud, to the perils and hazards of war; yet that national vanity, of which he so largely partakes, that prizes the renown of the soldier above all other needs of fame, incessantly urges him to enterprises for which his lack of resolute and determined courage otherwise disqualify him. His ridiculous assimilation of himself and fortunes to Napoleon, betrays alike the vanity and vaulting aspirations of the man. His sycophants are ever on the alert to discover and impart some resemblance between his mimicries of noble war, his little guerilla surprises, massacres, and murders, and the historic fields of the illustrious Corsican. He has thus been beguiled into filling his palace with every commemorated incident of the French campaigns; and rhapsodizes of destiny, with a weakness inconceivable in a man of his real superiority and ability. A monster of perfidy and hypocrisy—a vindictive tyrant and infidel—the foe to every form of freedom, but such as his own despotic will may accord—he has been by turns the champion and defender, the assailant and protector of religion, liberty, and humanity. At one time his country's benefactor, and at another its scourge, the caprices of his history and character baffle all conjecture as to his own destiny, or that of the government he has usurped. His popularity with his countrymen was so great, that thousands of prayers (we have been assured) went up to Heaven, from Mexican altars, whilst he was a prisoner of the Texans, that he would never be permitted to return! When the news of his release reached home, as many and fervent petitions were offered up that he would fall a victim to the fury of the mob in the United States, for his infamous murders at Goliad and Bexar. Many Mexicans there are who seriously allege that his escape from this latter retribution was solely owing to the national prejudice against Mexico, which spared their tyrant, that he might farther afflict his country. Thousands of persons mingled their congratulations in the capital and throughout the republic, that the amputation of his limb, shattered at Vera Cruz by the French, in 1838, would not save the monster's life; who, in 1842, united in the servile procession that received the disinterred leg at the gate of San Lazaro, and bore and buried it, amidst the most solemn ceremonials, in the cemetery of Santa Paula. He who, at the head of his veterans of Zacatecas, allowed himself to be surprised and captured by a handful of Texans, is now sung in ballads, and designated in the newspapers of the country, as *the Hero of San Jacinto!* He who again allowed himself to be surprised, and lost, by his negligence and cowardice, the Gibraltar of his country, to a handful of French marines and sailors, has an annual celebration instituted in his honour, for being accidentally hurt whilst peering out from behind the office of the portcaptain, at the retiring French, who had spiked the cannon and destroyed all the outworks of the city, committed him to defend. When justice had summoned him, as a peculator and traitor, before her tribunals, to answer for his corruptions and disloyalty, the very functionaries of his outraged country were seen vying with each other in their preparations of feasts and pageants to honour him within the towns, and grace his reception in the capital, where he came to be tried. One day he is suspected of urging the priesthood into a *pronunciamento* against his licentious soldiery, as enemies of public tranquillity and the security of the church; and on another he is found menacing this same clergy with a confiscation of their property to the uses of his soldiery, and a toleration of every form of Protestant service and creed.

A summary of his political history will best disclose the contempt for all principles and systems of which he is not the centre, entertained by this turbulent demagogue.

The Mexican revolution closed with the ascension of Iturbide to the imperial throne. Dissatisfied with his administration and the form of government he imposed, the Mexicans expelled him from the country in 1823, and calling a National Representative Congress, adopted, after a session of fourteen months, the memorable Federative system of 1824, with General Victoria as president. Various insurrections against this system occurred in favour of centralism, fomented by disappointed and ambitious chiefs, which were all suppressed, and the first federal administration closed auspiciously for the friends of freedom by the popular retirement of Victoria. The people then divided into two great parties: the Escossaises, who favoured a central form of government, and the Yorkinos, who supported the federal or existing system. In the second election which occurred, Gomez Pedraza, the central candidate, was elected by *two votes* over his opponent Guerrero, the Federal nominee. The Yorkinos, discontented with the success of Pedraza by so nominal a majority, denounced his election as a fraud; and Santa Anna heading the movement with a small body of followers, made his first bow on the political stage. The movement became popular, and after various skirmishes, the city of Mexico was captured by the insurgents, and given up to the sack and pillage of the mob. Pedraza, and such of his friends as could, made their escape, and flying the country took refuge abroad. A Congress was called by the victors, who proceeded to declare Guerrero to have been fairly elected, and Bustamente was elevated to the vice-presidency. The new President had scarcely been inaugurated before Bustamente retired to Japan, and organizing a military force in that city, pronounced against him, being soon after joined in the movement by Santa Anna. The revolution was successful; the president being defeated, and shortly after taken prisoner and executed as a traitor, at the instigation of Santa Anna. A few months previously Santa Anna had extinguished the last vestige of the Spanish power in Mexico by his renowned victory over Barrados at Tampico. Bustamente was installed in the presidency by Santa Anna and his victorious troops, and tranquillity once more restored to the country until 1832. Without a solitary reasonable pretext, this Mexican Warwick suddenly denounced Bustamente, and proclaimed himself in favour of the recall of the exiled Pedraza. A battle brought about a convention, by which Bustamente agreed to abdicate, and the fugitive Pedraza being brought back from the United States, where he had been residing, was sent to the capital to serve out the three months which remained of his unexpired term. This brief period was devoted by the grateful Pedraza to paving the way for the succession of his former foe, and late benefactor. Accordingly, Santa Anna was elevated to the supreme power, in the month of May, 1833.

Notwithstanding his high military reputation and popularity with both the soldiers and citizens, a central *pronunciamento* was fulminated against him early in his administration by Esculada, which being suppressed and the insurgents dispersed, his enthusiastic troops proceeded to proclaim him Dictator. This power and title he refused to assume, and soon after made a fresh popular display of his vigour and skill in subduing another insurrection under General Garcia, which had broke out in Zacatecas. Being now in universal favour, he secretly instigated and brought about the celebrated *pronunciamento* against the federal form of government (over which he presided, and in defence of which he had earned his laurels and power,) known in the history of the times, as the plan of Toluca. This plan utterly destroyed the constitution of 1824, vesting the supreme power in a central government, abolishing the state legislatures, and transposing the states themselves into departments, under the government of military commandants, responsible alone for the abuse of their authority, and dependent for the tenure of their office, on the executive and his cabinet. Under the name of the Central Constitution, it was adopted, and went into operation in 1836.

When fully assured of the success of this scheme of revolution, Santa Anna departed for Texas, with the flower of his conquering veterans, to put down the revolt in that province. Here the star of his destiny suffered its first eclipse, the invincible conqueror of Spaniards and Mexicans losing his army, liberty, and honour, and barely escaping with life itself, through the interference of the American executive.

Returning home, he lived buried in seclusion on his estates of Manga de Clavo, near Vera Cruz, an object of unmitigated scorn and contempt amongst his countrymen, until Bustamente, who had returned from France, and succeeded to the presidency under the new constitution, entrusted him with a command to repel the federal *emeute*, headed by General Mexia, in 1838. This he executed with such success, as to defeat Mexia in the most signal manner; dispersing and killing his entire force, and executing their captive leader, with attendant circumstances of cruelty, that tarnished as usual all the glory of his triumph. The succeeding winter, Vera Cruz was blockaded by a French fleet under Admiral Baudin, and the town and castle attacked by the troops. Santa Anna, who had been invested with the command of the force destined to protect it, attempted an unsuccessful surprise of the Prince de Joinville. His miscarriage was followed next morning by the counter surprise of himself and the garrison by the French, the Mexican general barely saving himself by escaping without coat, breeches, or hat, to his camp outside the town. The French, after spiking such cannon as they could not conveniently carry off, evacuated the town; and whilst reconnoitering their departure, he lost his leg as we have related. Again he retired to his estate, taking no part in public affairs until August, 1841, when the insurrection under Paredes broke out in Guadalaxaro, and being sustained by Santa Anna and several leading chiefs of the country, was ultimately terminated by the bombardment of the capital and a month's harmless conflict in the streets. Bustamente being overthrown, Santa Anna was chosen provisional president, and the Plan of Tacubaya adopted in lieu of the constitution. By this plan he was invested with dictatorial powers, and a Congress being assembled in June, 1842, to organize the government more fully, after intimating to them his wishes in regard to the organization, which they refused to acquiesce in, he dispersed them, and convened a Junta of Notables, for the purpose of carrying out his views. The deliberations of this Junta were proclaimed in June, 1843, whilst we were engaged upon the road between his palace and Tacubaya. It vests all power in the supreme central government, giving the president the full control of the army and navy, the whole patronage of the civil list, the regulation of the judiciary, a nearly unlimited veto on the acts of the Chamber of Deputies and Senate, composing the legislative power, and an overruling weight in the government, utterly at variance with the freedom of the people, or the independence of the rest of the departments.

By it the executive term is limited to five years, and Santa Anna had no difficulty in being confided with the possession of this his darling scheme of despotism. Whether his future efforts will be directed to entrench and fortify himself in power, or advance his country in its regeneration from ignorance, distraction, and misrule, remains to be seen.

Notwithstanding the abundance of her minerals, and the boundless fertility of her soil, the public debt of Mexico, incurred by her revolutions, and increased by the mismanagement of her resources, amounts to the enormous sum of eighty-four millions and a fraction of dollars. To pay the interest and instalments upon this indebtedness, and support the various branches of a government whose army alone cost, in 1840, eight millions of dollars, her whole annual revenue, ordinary and extraordinary, amounts to less than thirteen millions. Upon his accession to power, in 1841, Santa Anna found this debt impending over him, and not a dollar in the treasury with which to meet the daily wants and current expenses of the government. An army of thirty thousand men were to be maintained, the state in arrears to its civil officers, the copper currency of the realm debased sixty per cent., and, to swell his difficulties, dissensions prevailing amongst the troops and people, of the most threatening character. He met and overcame these embarrassments with a firmness and sagacity that reflects the utmost lustre upon his talents as a statesman. He has managed not only to maintain and enlarge his supreme power, in defiance of the machinations of his enemies, to pay his army and support his government, but to avert the most threatening difficulties with foreign powers, who held heavy claims against Mexico, the payment of whose principal and interest was necessarily suspended, and who were urging their demands under the menace of immediate war.

There is neither intelligence, energy, nor virtue amongst the masses of his countrymen sufficient to resist his encroachments upon their liberties; and the more enlightened and wealthy classes, tired of disorder and commotion, are supine under his usurpations, preferring the energy and vigour of his sway to the instability and insecurity of more liberal systems. The anarchy of party spirit in Mexico can only be prevented at present from rebaptizing the nation in blood by the powerful Prospero who raises, governs, and quells it at his pleasure.

Though maintaining a splendour far beyond any of his predecessors in government since the viceroys, in the style of his public state, Santa Anna is the impersonation of temperance and frugality in his private habits. But a solitary debasing vice of his countrymen seems to have found a place amongst his Spartan indulgences, and that so brutal and degrading, that it is thought he rather affects it, from its bloody and martial humour, than from any natural gusto he feels for it.

He is the proprietor of the most numerous and renowned strains of game-cocks to be found on the American continent, and is unremitting in his patronage of the blackguard sport, whenever his own birds are to take part in the contest. It is not an unusual spectacle to see him and his aide-de-camps attending the festivals at St. Augustine and elsewhere, and backing his cocks to the amount of thousands. Some dozen varieties of choice breeds of these fowls he brought home with him from the United States; and his obsequious courtiers not unfrequently tempt the paths to his patronage by romantic losses upon his favourite champions.

Chapter XV

*Tacubaya · The Egertons · Their mysterious
murder · Hopes of release · Santa Anna's alleged
reason for a refusal · Fourth of July, and petition for its
observance · Preparations for the fête · Stratagem to
supply our table · Oration and other ceremonies
of the day · Conclusion of the fête.*

Tacubaya, beside its vicinity to the summer residence of the Mexican court, is distinguished as the favourite retreat of the wealthy merchants of the capital, many of them having delightful and highly improved country villas in and around this village, where their families reside a greater portion of the year. It is about a mile from Chapultepec, (the cherished home of the emperors of the Mexican empire,) and is entrenched in gardens and grottoes, and surrounded by all that nature and art can contribute to embellish it.

In 1842, it was the scene of one of those dismal and mysterious assassinations, whose foulness and brutality is without a parallel in savage cruelty. Mr. Egerton, an English painter of eminent talent, who had spent several years in Mexico, prosecuting his art in sketching its unrivalled scenery, revisited his native land, and after a brief absence, returned with a young, lovely, and accomplished companion, to share the raptures of his tropical home. Of reserved habits, and a refined taste, that made its chief enjoyment in the smiles of love, and witchery of the world around him, he sought refuge amongst the quiet bowers of Tacubaya, where, in a cottage consecrated to peace and the tenderest transports, some glowing months passed off, in ecstacies unmitigated by any presence but the ministry of the joyous hours. Abandoned to the intoxicating bliss of their little paradise, the enamoured pair never left it, but to wander from nook to nook of the beautiful landscape that girdled them, awaking the noonday silence of its groves with music, or watching amidst its purple sunsets the snow-ruffled volcanoes around, as fold after fold they flung their broad curtain of shadow over the plain below.

From such an evening's excursion, the poodle of the lady (the solitary companion of their rambles,) returned alone to the cottage late at night, and the alarm being given by their servants, a search was instituted on the following morning that resulted in the discovery of the bodies of the murdered lovers. Our sentinel, who related the sad particulars, and who was himself present at the discovery, described the spectacle (though twelve months had intervened since he saw it), with a horror of expression that faithfully corroborated the revolting atrocity of his narrative.

On the side of a retired road that led out through the fields towards a sequestered chapel, the body of the hapless artist was found, pierced with numberless sword-wounds, and mangled with blows from bludgeons. It lay where it had fallen, the ploughed and blood-sprinkled earth around testifying the struggle had been a severe one. His cane still clenched with tenacity in the rigid grip of death, his stiffened hair, clenched teeth, and distended eyes; his knit brow and compressed lips, all bore terrible witness to the desperate conflict he had waged with his ambushed butchers.

A further examination discovered in a neighbouring thicket the lifeless and dishonoured form of her, who was so lately the tutelary divinity of his solitary worship, the solace of his exile, the sharer of his blissful Eden, the idol of his endearments, and fellow-victim of his ruthless destroyers. The white foam of madness was upon her writhed lips, her eyes strained and started from their sockets, her long silken hair torn and trampled in the sward, and her pale spectral fingers clasped as though, when love and courage had sunk overpowered at her side, her anguished soul had sought shelter from farther ruin in fruitless appeals of pity. Stripped naked of every article of clothing but her shoes and stockings, two gory spots to the right and left below her breasts disclosed where the rapier had been driven through her body, whilst her bitten bosom, and the empurpled marks of ruffian fingers round her throat, were added to other indisputable proofs of her violation.

All Mexico rang with horror, excited by the perpetration of this execrable deed. The numerous peasantry around, and crowds from Tacubaya, drawn to the spot, wept and shuddered over the forlorn and blasted remains of the gifted and devoted strangers. The British minister and consul sought the instant presence of the government, and demanded with fierce indignation its most prompt and vigorous assistance in the apprehension and punishment of the guilty. The government did employ its utmost energies and perseverance in the discovery. Heavy rewards were proclaimed, and all ranks and classes united with alacrity in the search. Person after person was arrested, examined, and dismissed, and resort had to England itself, for some clue to the tragedy; but nothing whatever has been elicited to the present hour, which can throw light on the cause that provoked, or the monsters who acted as the ministers of the outrage.

A cross of the rudest craftsmanship near the thicket where they suffered, marks the site of the atrocity, and a Latin inscription implores the prayers of the passing faithful for the souls of the murdered heretics.

We had been induced by the representations of friends and Mexican officers high in rank, to look forward with some degree of confidence to being liberated on the 13th of June, the day of publication of the new constitution by the Junta of Notables, and still more sacred as the birthday of the usurper. This day, it was suggested, had been fixed on by the Dictator (the great *beneficiary* of that instrument), as one of general jubilee, when the prisons throughout the realm were to be thrown open, and amnesty granted for all past offences. But the day came and past, and whatever advantages accrued from it to others, none lighted on our heads. The reason alleged by Santa Anna for refusing our promised freedom, was the intelligence he had received of the ill-starred expedition of Snively and Warfield, against Santa Fe.

The 4th of July, the sacramental day of American independence, having arrived, a memorial to the president was drawn up and presented by a committee of our officers, in behalf of the prisoners; petitioning a respite from labour on that day, with the farther privilege of being allowed to celebrate it in the spirit and after the fashion of our American sires. The Dictator was much embarrassed for a while in what manner to treat the application, but yielded at length an assent, accompanied by the declaration, that the privilege was accorded, from his *unbounded reverence for the signers of that heroic pronunciamento, rather than from any respect for their unworthy descendants,* who asked to observe it. Without bandying more words with such an insolent sarcasm on freedom and patriotism, the committee returned to quarters, and we all straightway set about preparing for the glorious occasion.

After the various committees had been appointed, and an orator selected, we were nonplussed for a copy of the Declaration of Independence; and the committee of ways and means, to whose lot it fell to provide suitable viands and refreshments, found the resources of the *gang* utterly inadequate to the emergency. It was in vain every pocket was religiously emptied of its last *claco*, and the proceeds of the chains and tools we had sold delivered over with scrupulous exactness. The whole amount when collected and counted over was scarce sufficient to procure the ham and whiskey, so indispensable to rouse that patriotic jollity, without which the feast of reason and flow of soul slumbers under the sublimest skill of bard or rhetorician. In this dilemma, we were fain to adopt the suggestion of a Yankee comrade, and invite the despot's slaves to unite in the celebration. The invitations were accordingly made out to the officers of our guard, and couched in such pompous flourishes of stilty Mexican courtesy, as brought assurances of their grateful acceptance of the honour from every epauletted hero to whom they were addressed. Colonel Rangel, our superintendent, insisted on catering for the table, and various presents came in from anonymous donors, of pulque, brandy, fruit, fowls, and fish, that elevated our esteem of Mexican generosity to the very acme of enthusiasm. The largest room of the old mill was assigned us as the scene for the festive banquet; our committee of sculptors having failed in several busts of Washington and Jefferson they attempted, the walls of the hall were forthwith decorated with charcoal designs and portraits, that reflected the brightest lustre on the pictorial genius of the delineators.

A diminutive piece of brass ordnance was sent down from the barracks, to usher in the glorious morning with the customary salutes for every state of the confederacy, but either through design or ignorance, their cartridges gave out at nine, and we were accordingly compelled to acquiesce in this dogmatical retrenchment of the sovereignties of the Union. Our president and vice presidents, toast-readers and orator, were all, unfortunately, in chains; and upon consultation, it was thought most appropriate they should thus appear, as calculated at one and the same time to portray the hideousness of tyranny, and heighten the effects of those denunciatory sentiments intended to be pronounced.

At two o'clock precisely, our guests being arrived, we sat down to three sumptuous and loaded tables, groaning under every variety of well-prepared dishes. Jugs, bowls, and bottles of enlivening admixtures, were plentifully interspersed between, whilst, from ceiling and walls, sooty etchings and mottoes looked down, commemorative of the cherished country and hallowed anniversary we kept. Reversing the usual order of these entertainments, we postponed the inspiring felicities of national glorification to the more substantial delights spread around us, and mutely prosecuted the extension of liberty and truth over the world by furious and unremitting assaults upon the flagon and trencher. Gaily we plied our guests, and most prodigally helped ourselves, forgetful, after repeated potations, that the gallant strangers were other than coheirs with us in the hereditary renown we were appropriating. A decorous silence was for some time kept up; but as the feast progressed, some of our fellows, touched with the *long absent filter,* talked of their own prowess, and the trophied deeds of their sires, muttered of their martyred comrades, and defied the field and scaffold, for the holy cause of their country and its rights. Others brewed little courtesies in Spanish, and addressed them to our guests in reiterated salutations of *Buenos dias, cabelleros, espero que la veo en perfecta salud*—concluding with a leer, and the affectionate inquiries of *Como está su señor hermano? su señora? su madre? su madrasta i suegro?* in rapid succession. By and by, having done amplest justice to the good cheer, and the carnival becoming more free and unrestrained, it was demanded that the oration in honour of the sanctified spirits (*supposed* to be) hovering over us, be delivered. There being no cloth to remove, and the orator seeming properly fired up and ready for the onset, was called out amidst deafening acclamations. Judge Gibson, who had been honoured with this prominent part in the services, overcome with emotions excited by the novelty and peculiarity of the circumstances under which he was to discharge it, hesitated for some minutes after rising, and looking round upon the throng of curious and upturned faces, stammered out an opening sentence and was silent. In a breath, fifty familiar prompters were offering him as many different exordiums, interlarded with injunctions from others, of *Give it to the tyrant*—*Contrast him with Washington*—*Refresh them with San Jacinto*—*Remember the Alamo*—*Don't forget Mier!* and such like uproarious intimations of their various wishes as caused the Mexicans present to half rise from their seats, as apprehensive of outrage. Silence, however, was restored, and the most cordial assurances of continued tranquillity given by the president to the guests. The speaker, gathering composure to proceed, dashed off over human rights and sceptred despotism—chivalric sires and undegenerate sons—bleeding patriots and hireling invaders—desecrated altars—monumental tombs—baffled navies and captive armies—with thrilling allusion to the triumphs and disasters—sufferings and achievements, of those who barred them in the holy cause of freedom's first matchless and victorious rally upon the western continent.

As he reviewed the history of the American Revolution, and portrayed the loyalty, sacrifices, and valour of the immortal band who brought it to a successful conclusion, peals of applause and stamping of feet, acompanied by a fiendlike clanking of chains, testified the approval of his delighted audience. But when he came to refer to the canonized memory and holy fame of the illustrious father of his country, the raptures of our elevated and enthusiastic comrades overleaped all bounds of restraint. Some shouted in the defiant tones of a forlorn hope mounting a deadly breach, some beat the table boards, alternately with their knuckles and fetters, whilst a few of the more active bacchanals whisked upon the table itself, and, clearing a space of the platters and their contents, regaled themselves with hornpipes, backsteps, and slop-shuffles, as their Terpsichorian training permitted. Amidst the din of this sublime outburst our noble guests retired, and the orator, turning his back upon the uproarious portion of the assembly, continued his harangue to a select coterie of the more staid and rational, until he had exhausted his powers and subject.

The regular toasts, which had been prepared for the occasion, were attempted to be read, but were clamoured down, as too dull and cold, and volunteer substitutes culled from brains seething with fun, fury, and frenzy, bawled out at the highest pitch of voice by the Hampdens and Sydneys of the revel. Songs of jollity, patriotism, and sentiment, were trolled in open contempt of all orchestral canons; List, dear Lady, and Hail Columbia—Twilight Dews and Starspangled Banner, mounting and mingling with each other in the most charming confusion.

A file of sentinels entered about six o'clock, and, marching us off to the measure and chorus of the Marseilles Hymn, locked us up to dream off the mists of the wine-cup. A few minutes after their retirement, and overpowered with sleep, we were traversing the familiar paths of happier days,—

"Hearing our own mountain-goats bleating aloft,
And soothed with the strain that the corn-reapers sung."

Chapter XVI

*Escape of nine prisoners · Release of
Dr. —— · His unpopularity · Holidays
and their amusements amongst the prisoners ·
Private dinner given us by the ladies · Beauty and
kindness of our entertainers · Return to Santiago · Get
rid of our irons · Route through the valley, and view
of it from the mountains · Rio Frio and its
bandits · Haciendas and volcanoes.*

Nine of our men, viz., Copelin, Walker, Gattis, Wilson, Day, Craw-
ford, Thompson, Fitzgerald, and Daugherty, became impatient,
whilst labouring here, to revisit their homes, and decamped without
the slightest ceremony of leaves-taking. All but Daugherty went
away at night; he strolling off at broad noonday, with as much *nonchalance* as though he bore a formal discharge and regular passport
under the president's own signature. A terrible commotion ensued
when their departure was discovered; platoons of cavalry being
despatched in all directions in quest of them; their names and descriptions of their persons gazetted, and the police of the capital
urged to the most thorough examination of the various lurks of its
suburbs. No tidings reached us of the fate of any but Copelin, who
was retaken near Matamoras, about a month after his elopement,
and brought back to Perote.

Many more would have followed their example, and embraced the
frequent opportunities presented them, but for unintermitted assurances from friends of our speedy liberation. Besides, but the fewest
number had a solitary vestment beyond the notorious garb they
wore, which must have led to their immediate detection, wherever
they presented themselves. Nor had we money; and we recoiled
from farther taxing the liberality of those who had already extended
us such generous aid, or involving them in the consequences of a
connivance in our flight.

To our mutual gratification, we got rid of Dr. ——— here, being the worthy who brought us the white flag at Mier, and who was ever after execrated by the men for urging our surrender, when he knew (or ought to have known) the meditated retreat by Ampudia, had we refused his offer. Conscious of the odium in which he was held, he sought to resent it by a base neglect of such of the soldiers as were dependent upon his aid; suffering them to die in the same room with himself, for the want of those services they were too destitute to command.

The numerous holidays observed by the Mexicans extend to their soldiers, and on such occasions, locking us in for the day and mounting a few sentries over us, the rest of the guard betook themselves to the neighbouring towns to enjoy the festivities.

One of these lock-up days being that on which the elections in Texas were held, we amused ourselves by a nomination of opposing candidates for the offices of senator and representatives in Congress. The nominations were followed by a most animating canvass, speeches being made, offices and treats promised, and all the cajoleries and strategie of a genuine and heated contest observed. There was no fighting, tippling, or pipe-laying, but considerable crowding and swearing at the polls, and challenges of votes, for more sensible reasons than many of the established restrictions of the inestimable right of suffrage. Judge Gibson, the orator of the 4th, was elected by a slim majority to the Senate, and Captain Buster, who had shortly before joined us, by a more complimentary one, to the House; neither, however, reached home in time to claim their seats.

One day, at the completion of our forenoon's task, we were abruptly formed and marched off in a direction opposite to that of our quarters, no explanation whatever being vouchsafed us of our destination, or the objects of the movement. Arriving on the bank of the little stream that skirts the village, we found in a grove of stately ash a long table spread with a most substantial and abundant repast. Seats to it were being placed by servants, under the superintendence of the most beautiful and exquisitely-dressed ladies we had encountered in our wanderings through Mexico. They were the wives and daughters of the opulent French, English, American, and Mexican merchants of Tacubaya, who had obtained permission from Santa Anna to bestow the luxury of a good dinner upon us in this picnic form. Nothing could be finer than the *ensemble* of the lovely group; the most graceful effect of contrast being presented in the

varieties of their style and appearance. The dark brunette skins, liquid and vivacious eyes, raven-black and glossy tresses, voluptuous symmetry, and stately magnificent tread, of the Mexican señoras and donzellas, robed in rich-coloured petticoats, and draped in the coquettish folds of lace mantillas or embroidered shawls, were in high relief with the chiselled features and tinted blonde complexions, modest costume, and chaste expression, of their European and American companions. There was quite as much difference in the character of sympathy that looked out from our kind entertainers upon the rude and friendless subjects of their hospitality. After being seated, the Mexican and French women drew near us, and seemed engrossed with the tenderest solicitude that every needful provision had been made for our wants, stimulating the relish of their viands by graceful ministrations of service, and the most gentle expressions of pity for our misfortunes. Their soft and compassionate eyes seemed actually to bid us eat, and run away from their brutal countrymen. The American ladies and their Saxon kindred stood aloof from our board, eyeing us with a sad and humiliated look, as though a common national origin involved them to some degree in the degradation of our lot. Their scrutiny of our squalid line was one of mingled sorrow and mortification, and we felt under their earnest and thoughtful glances, a sting of wounded pride, that gladly sought shelter in the more active and unreproving humanities of their associates of the day.

A scrupulous propriety marked the deportment of our fellows on this occasion, and notwithstanding the spell of the refined presence that surrounded them, they acquitted themselves in the most creditable manner towards the attractions set before them. After a suitable acknowledgment of our gratitude, delivered in Spanish, to the kind projectors of the feast, we retired to our drudgery on the road.

After a few days more, this highway, which had occupied us four months in making, was completed, and orders given on the 9th of September to pack up for a return to Santiago. In an hour after receiving them we were all ready for the way, and being chained in the fashion in which we arrived here, set out for the old convent, which we reached a little before dark. All farther thoughts of an immediate liberation were extinguished in our bosoms, by information from Colonel Rangel that we were destined for Perote.

We were detained but two days at Santiago, when we were called up on the morning of the 12th to have our irons cut off, preparatory

to setting out for our resident prison. This was a needless preliminary as it turned out, each man in obedience to the summons throwing off his incumbrances as easily as though his body had shrunk to
the dimensions of a skeleton. The smith, a burly soot-covered Mexican, stared and grinned with astonishment as one by one the subjects on which he was called to exercise his art, approached his
block, and giving the bolt of the clevis that embraced their ankles
a touch, dropped the shackles at his feet, and walked off. Whilst at
Tacubaya, though we were compelled to wear them during the day,
no one ever thought of sleeping in them, kicking them off like old
shoes the very moment the key was turned on us. The first hail of
the sentinel next morning, and all were refettered as securely as
before.

Twenty of our men being too sick for the road, were left behind
here; and, under a strong cavalry escort, and a brilliant sun that lit
up the beautiful valley from its midst to its mountain boundaries,
we pursued our way towards Perote. From the rising grounds we ascended towards evening, we caught a last prospect of the gorgeous
city, reposing in the centre of its enchanted landscape, like some
mammoth diamond in the brilliant tiara of royalty. No description
of the pen or pencil can ever faithfully portray, (much less exagger-
ate,) the elemental grandeur and beauty of sky, plain, mountain,
lake, grove, and garden, grouped together in this little world of ter-
restrial loveliness. It may lack the curling smoke, the motion and
hum of life, the vitality of the panoramas of the old world, but there
is a magic of peace and poetry in the stillness of its picture, that
melts on the heart, and falls like dreamy whispers on the senses,
making it more fanciful and graceful as it is.

Our route through the day was along a low range of volcanic hills,
that border the highway leading from the city towards Vera Cruz,
flanked by fields of grain and agave, and dotted at intervals with
hamlets and isolated chapels. An elevated causeway, constructed by
the Spaniards, extends about seven miles from the capital, through
a marshy vegetable flat, reported as the ancient bed of Tezcuco, but
from which its waters have long since receded. Myriads of wild-
fowls still inhabit either side of the dike, and are slaughtered in immense quantities for the Mexican market.

Groups of dirty, ragged Indians, some with empty chicken-coops
on their heads, and others driving half-starved asses loaded with
panniers and children, loitered on the road returning from market,

drinking, singing, and sleeping, or hailing us with offers of refuse fruit and vegetables, in open contempt of the threats and interdict of the guard. One fellow plodded towards the city with water-fowls suspended from his neck to his knees, followed by his docile and greasy spouse, with their youngest responsibility on her back, and a thrifty troop at her heels, carrying on their heads and shoulders the simple implements of their outdoor household and cookery. At our encampment some twenty-four miles on the road, we were overtaken by two American friends from the capital, Messrs. Pratt and Walker, who had come out to bid us adieu, and extend at parting some additional services to the many generous and liberal aids they had previously bestowed on us.

Ten miles farther brought us to the eastern barrier of the valley, where, toiling for hours up a road heaped with stones, and ploughed into gullies by the descending torrents, we at length reached the summit, some two thousand feet above the plain. Towering and dark-looking pines fringe the mountain sides from base to top, and from out their solemn shades peer at every turn of the serpentine way, those sepulchral crosses, that mark the sites of ancient and recent murders. From this eminence the eye may pierce through the pure and vapourless air across the opposing summits of the western range, and pursuing a billowy sea of mountain and valley beyond, follow up the expanded view until it melts away into the dim and cloudless horizon. From out the solitudes of the surrounding forests came shrill and biting winds, that moaned amongst the echoing boughs with the discordant tones of a rising tempest.

Descending the mountain on its eastern slope by frequent and circuitous windings, we reached at sundown the narrow and gloomy ravine, ploughed by a brawling brook, upon whose banks is situated a wretched cluster of hovels called Rio Frio.

The only occupation of the wild and desperate villains who inhabit them is charcoal burning; and their savage appearance and surly habits, together with the numerous assassinations and robberies in the vicinity, have procured them the reputation of being the most noted and formidable bandits in Mexico. A constant intelligence is maintained between their villages and comrades in the mountains; and every facility thus afforded for plundering the passing traveller and diligence, when the booty of either may tempt their cupidity. Sullenly and reluctantly they pointed out to the guard a dirty hut for our night's accommodation, nor could bribes or commands procure us beyond the most stinted supply of food to stay the fierce appetites excited by our march. They permitted us to traverse their fastness, however, without the compliment of robbing us; an indignity we resented next morning, by seizing several asses from them to mount our men, who had fallen lame on the previous day.

Continuing our descent of the mountains for the greater part of the next day, we emerged at length from its wild and untilled labyrinths into plains of gentle inclination, containing extensive and highly cultivated estates. These large haciendas, with their principal mansion, chapel, and numerous outhouses, resemble through the foliage so many tasteful villages gleaming out from the surrounding groves. Numerous flocks of sheep, and herds of cattle and horses, grazed over the immense meadows; and fine streams at intervals dashed along the plains, crossed by bridges of the most solid and costly masonry. To the right of the road, in the distance, rose the gigantic peaks of the rival volcanoes, Popocatepetl, and Iztaccihuatl, clad in their snowy mantles, and towering majestically far above the stupendous range to which they belong. Night overtook us as we reached the little village of San Martin, where, hungry and weary, we found the welcome rarities of an excellent supper and tolerable quarters.

Chapter XVII

Aspect of the country near Puebla ·
Indian family · Republics of Tlascala,
Cholula, and Huexotzingo · Pyramid of Cholula ·
Puebla de los Angelos · Convent Alameda, Plaza and
Cathedral · Female felon · Manufactories
of Puebla.

We were off from St. Martin by the dawn, a nipping chilling north-easter whistling in our faces, making the officers of our guard draw their serapes tightly around them. When the sun came up, the winds fell to the gentlest breathing, and we jogged along the level elevation of the plain with steps almost elastic.

As we neared Puebla, the country continued to improve in appearance and tillage; single fields containing more than a thousand acres spread out before us, and planted in maize or maguey. The haciendas, too, became more elegant and numerous, and groups of labourers, and heavy oxcarts with hewn timber wheels, passed us in the direction of their employments.

Under a clump of shade trees that fronted an isolated hut some fifty yards from the road-side, lolled an indolent Indian family, engaged in the primitive occupation of searching each other's heads. Some five or six children of either sex were thus affectionately employed; and the mother, a tall and portly-looking woman, pursued the delicate operation on a dark-eyed and voluptuous daughter of some sixteen summers. The object of this tender solicitude sat at her mother's feet, replaiting the strands of her inky hair, into the long queue, so much in vogue amongst their caste. In no degree embarrassed by our appearance, the girl remained passive; her ruffled chemise flung open in front, and gaudy cotton petticoat drawn up to her knees, riveted her great liquid eyes upon our detachment as it passed, with the *naïve* and unabashed stare of a young ballet-dancer.

Chapter XVII

The father, a puncheon-shaped old gentleman, sat squatted on his
ns some few yards removed from his domestic circle, strumming
ndoline as gaily as though he were proprietor or administrador
st of the adjoining hacienda. As we turned an angle of the road
hundred yards farther, the little and picturesque figure of the
us undulating in a slow and languid measure to her father's
nd (we may suppose) her partial mother's admiration. Some
of the rear guard wheeling their horses round the better to
late her movements, she suddenly stopped, then nodding
in token of being observed, and waving the reboso she held
id in coquettish salutations, continued her solitary fan-

le-lands of Puebla, over which we were journeying, are
thousand feet above the sea, and, besides a climate of
are esteemed the most fertile soil in Mexico. Wheat,
guey, are their principal staples, and abundant crops
of fruit mingle in their productions. Their ancient
arly across the country, having formerly embraced
invincible republics of Tlascala, Cholula, and Hu-
powerful and defensive league held the Mexican
und aided the Spaniards in its ultimate conquest
he capital of the former, once the opulent rival
e, is now a wretched ruin, all traces of its van-
ing gone but the walls of its majestic temple.
l city, and metropolis of the second republic,
nd dwellings, and four hundred temples, Cortes
narch he had himself counted,) has likewise fallen
quest to a heap of hovels, containing a population at
ess than six thousand souls. The pyramid of this name,
t memorable relic to antiquaries on the American continent,
few miles to the west of Puebla, and has been visited and
ibed by every traveller of note who has interested himself in
antiquities of the country. It rises sudden and unassociated from
e midst of the plain, built in pyramidal form, of adobes or large
nburned bricks, and though mutilated and overgrown with trees,
the massive base and four stories of the monument are nearly entire.
Humboldt describes it as a work of such magnitude and vastness as,
next to the Pyramids of Egypt, approaches nearest the mighty creations of nature. Its height is one hundred and seventy-two feet, and
the sides of its base one thousand three hundred and fifty-five, being

two hundred and seventy-six feet lower than the great Pyramid
Cheops, and six hundred and twenty-seven longer. The brick ma
ial is interspersed with layers of stone and plaster, and the
stories connected with each other by terraces. These again a
cended from bench to bench by regular and oblique flights of
cut by the old Spaniards, as a way to a little chapel on the pl
dedicated to the Virgin of *Remedios*. In straightening the ro
Mexico to Puebla, it became necessary to traverse a portio
base, when the section laid open an interior chamber, buil
and roofed with beams of cypress. In it were found skelet
of basalt, and a number of vases curiously varnished and

Many are the conjectures of the savants who have exa
to the original design of this edifice, or the uses to whi
voted by the aborigines. Whether it was intended as
tomb, a palace or a place of sepulchre, may long cont
the curious, who delight to grope in the gloom of th
are not sure that the fruits of their research will exc
of the simple Mexican, who frankly replies to the
purposes, "*Quien sabe?*"–Who knows, or who can

Mexico abounds with pyramids of more or less
various elevations, from its plains to its mountai
Indian traditions and legends respecting them
their construction to the gods and demigods of
ology.

A forest of spires and domes bathed in the rich
ting sun, and jutting above spacious squares of
proclaimed the presence of the second most sple
ing city of the republic, Puebla de los Angelos.

On the western side, where we entered, an enormous
and lofty buildings embrace the convent of St. Francis, fro
the fashionable and graceful walks of the Alameda, from
avenues of retired shade, poured out a lengthening throng of
and dons, gallant cavaliers and flashing donzellas. Passing ove
broad, well-paved, and cleanly streets, crossing each other at ri
angles, and walled on every side by stately edifices, we entered o
gloomy prison, amidst the dying chimes of innumerable bells, cal
ing the devout to their vesper orisons.

The following day, (September 16th,) being the festival of their
political independence, was celebrated throughout the country with
the utmost pomp and parade, and that our guard might not be de-

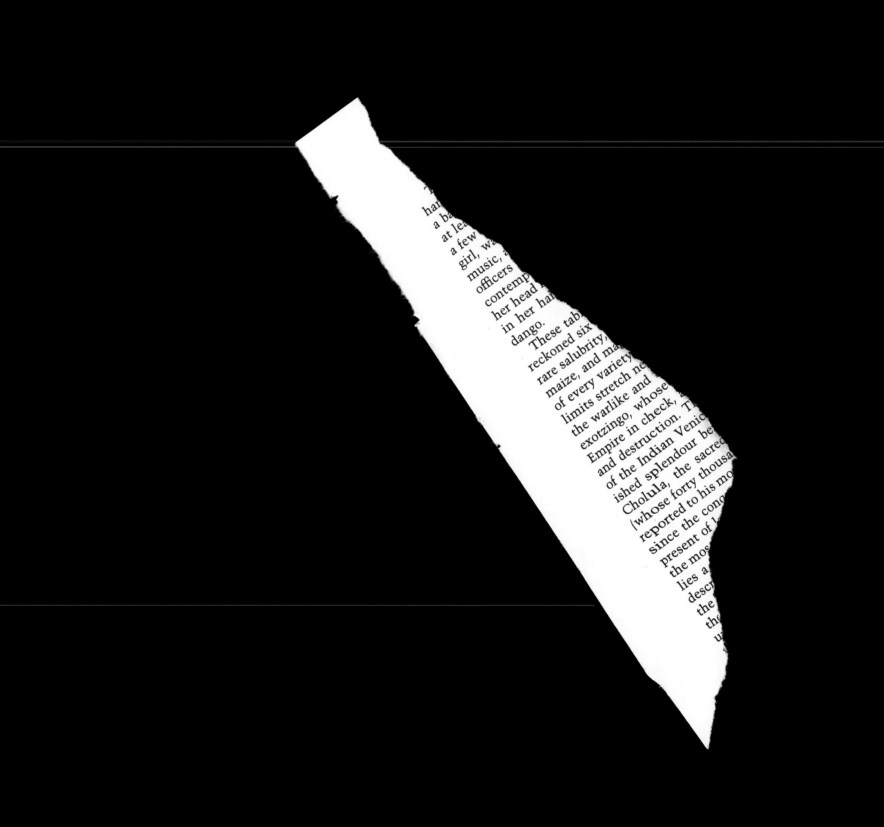

T
ha
a ba
at lea
a few
girl, wa
music,
officers
contemp
her head
in her ha
dango.
These tab
reckoned six
rare salubrity,
maize, and ma
of every variety
limits stretch ne
the warlike and
exotzingo, whose
Empire in check,
and destruction. T
of the Indian Venic
ished splendour be
Cholula, the sacred
(whose forty thousa
reported to his mo
since the conq
present of
the mos
lies a
descr
the
th
u

d of
ter-
four
e as-
steps,
atform,
ad from
n of the
c of stone
ons, idols
painted.
mined it, as
ch it was de-
a temple or a
nue to puzzle
e past, but we
eed the wisdom
inquirer after its
tell?
grandeur, found at
summits, and the
unite in ascribing
their ample myth-

gilding of the set-
turretted masonry,
endid and flourish-

nile of large
onted by
whose
ames
the
ight
ur
l-

The father, a puncheon-shaped old gentleman, sat squatted on his hams some few yards removed from his domestic circle, strumming a bandoline as gaily as though he were proprietor or administrador at least of the adjoining hacienda. As we turned an angle of the road a few hundred yards farther, the little and picturesque figure of the girl, was undulating in a slow and languid measure to her father's music, and (we may suppose) her partial mother's admiration. Some officers of the rear guard wheeling their horses round the better to contemplate her movements, she suddenly stopped, then nodding her head in token of being observed, and waving the reboso she held in her hand in coquettish salutations, continued her solitary fandango.

These table-lands of Puebla, over which we were journeying, are reckoned six thousand feet above the sea, and, besides a climate of rare salubrity, are esteemed the most fertile soil in Mexico. Wheat, maize, and maguey, are their principal staples, and abundant crops of every variety of fruit mingle in their productions. Their ancient limits stretch nearly across the country, having formerly embraced the warlike and invincible republics of Tlascala, Cholula, and Huexotzingo, whose powerful and defensive league held the Mexican Empire in check, and aided the Spaniards in its ultimate conquest and destruction. The capital of the former, once the opulent rival of the Indian Venice, is now a wretched ruin, all traces of its vanished splendour being gone but the walls of its majestic temple. Cholula, the sacred city, and metropolis of the second republic, (whose forty thousand dwellings, and four hundred temples, Cortes reported to his monarch he had himself counted,) has likewise fallen since the conquest to a heap of hovels, containing a population at present of less than six thousand souls. The pyramid of this name, the most memorable relic to antiquaries on the American continent, lies a few miles to the west of Puebla, and has been visited and described by every traveller of note who has interested himself in the antiquities of the country. It rises sudden and unassociated from the midst of the plain, built in pyramidal form, of adobes or large unburned bricks, and though mutilated and overgrown with trees, the massive base and four stories of the monument are nearly entire. Humboldt describes it as a work of such magnitude and vastness as, next to the Pyramids of Egypt, approaches nearest the mighty creations of nature. Its height is one hundred and seventy-two feet, and the sides of its base one thousand three hundred and fifty-five, being two hundred and seventy-six feet lower than the great Pyramid of Cheops, and six hundred and twenty-seven longer. The brick material is interspersed with layers of stone and plaster, and the four stories connected with each other by terraces. These again are ascended from bench to bench by regular and oblique flights of steps, cut by the old Spaniards, as a way to a little chapel on the platform, dedicated to the Virgin of *Remedios*. In straightening the road from Mexico to Puebla, it became necessary to traverse a portion of the base, when the section laid open an interior chamber, built of stone and roofed with beams of cypress. In it were found skeletons, idols of basalt, and a number of vases curiously varnished and painted.

Many are the conjectures of the savants who have examined it, as to the original design of this edifice, or the uses to which it was devoted by the aborigines. Whether it was intended as a temple or a tomb, a palace or a place of sepulchre, may long continue to puzzle the curious, who delight to grope in the gloom of the past, but we are not sure that the fruits of their research will exceed the wisdom of the simple Mexican, who frankly replies to the inquirer after its purposes, "*Quien sabe?*"—Who knows, or who can tell?

Mexico abounds with pyramids of more or less grandeur, found at various elevations, from its plains to its mountain summits, and the Indian traditions and legends respecting them unite in ascribing their construction to the gods and demigods of their ample mythology.

A forest of spires and domes bathed in the rich gilding of the setting sun, and jutting above spacious squares of turretted masonry, proclaimed the presence of the second most splendid and flourishing city of the republic, Puebla de los Angelos.

On the western side, where we entered, an enormous pile of large and lofty buildings embrace the convent of St. Francis, fronted by the fashionable and graceful walks of the Alameda, from whose avenues of retired shade, poured out a lengthening throng of dames and dons, gallant cavaliers and flashing donzellas. Passing over the broad, well-paved, and cleanly streets, crossing each other at right angles, and walled on every side by stately edifices, we entered our gloomy prison, amidst the dying chimes of innumerable bells, calling the devout to their vesper orisons.

The following day, (September 16th,) being the festival of their political independence, was celebrated throughout the country with the utmost pomp and parade, and that our guard might not be debarred so patriotic an indulgence, we were informed we should not leave our quarters till the ensuing morning. At an early hour, continued roars of artillery announced the advent of the joyful epoch; whilst throughout the forenoon, peals of national music, tolling bells, and the ascension of numerous rockets and balloons, witnessed the activity with which the festivities were conducted. It was impossible to repress a smile at the eagerness and enthusiasm with which the Mexican convicts, from the court of the prison, listened and watched for these evidences of the hilarity of their countrymen outside. A bandy-legged, grizzle-haired old covey, fresh from the highway, with his wrists and ankles heavily manacled, and who (his companions informed us) would be certainly garrotted, for a late excursion on the road, would throw up his fettered arms, and clamour his shrill bravos, whenever a *bomba de carton*, or *cohete*, mounted in view. *"Por el amor del Santo Jesus,"* he would cry, whilst his eyes flashed with ecstacy, *"Mira la magnifica bomba, el bravo cohete, mira como relampaguéa, pegara el cielo!*

Through the interest of a young officer of the guard, who had been a prisoner in Texas, two of us were permitted to accompany him in an afternoon's ramble through the city, and at three o'clock we passed out of the prison with our guide, and circuited a number of the beautiful squares.

The streets were teeming with population, great numbers having been attracted from the country and the neighbouring towns by the celebration of the day. The balconies and open windows blushed with their blooming flowers and lovely women, and the lofty walls of the rooms, into which we could see, were covered with rich-looking pictures and costly mirrors. Old monks and young friars, in their broad shovel hats and canonical habits, nuns, modistes, and fruit-girls, and the regular lords of the *pavé*, from *millionaire* to *leperos*, jostled each other on the crowded footways. In the centre of the city is the great *plaza*, built up on two sides by houses on arches, which answer as thoroughfares for the *entrée* and exit of the crowds who haunt it. To the north stands the palace of the governor, and to the south again is the vast pile of the cathedral, amongst the richest and most finished pieces of ecclesiastical architecture in the world. In the splendour and endowments of her numerous churches and conventual establishments Puebla is unsurpassed by any city in Christendom; but her cathedral is the boast and pride of her people; and truly does it merit all the admiration they bestow.

The exterior, neither in ornament nor tasteful execution, strikes the beholder as corroborating the sacred ministration employed in its erection. A monkish legend represents, whilst it was in the course of building, the angels of God came down at night, and added as much to the work as the masons had performed through the day. Hence the sobriquet *de los Angelos* to the city name.

The material is a light blue stone, dressed in heavy blocks, solidly jointed, and supported by immense buttresses, that terminate at the west in lofty towers, filled with large and clear-toned bells. Here is the main entrance, and overhead several subjects of scriptural history sculptured in stone. Within the miracle displays itself to its full advantage.

Rows of massive columns, with plinths and capitals of burnished gold, divide the nave of the church into three departments, outside of which, to the right and left, are sunken arches, leading to small chapels embedded in the wall, and railed off by gates of iron. From the centre of the immense dome depends a gigantic chandelier of gold and silver, whose enormous mass is computed at many tons weight. The altar is built of beautiful marbles, of every variety of colour and cost, and beneath its elevated platform is the circular sepulchre of the bishops, covered over by a depressed dome, and lighted by silver lamps, which, like the sacred fires of the vestals, are never suffered to be extinguished. Surrounding this platform are lofty candelabras of solid silver and gold, which light the altar; and above, in a double chapel, opened and shut by concealed machinery, is the host, blazing with rare and priceless jewels.

The most striking object of the interior is a life-sized figure of the Virgin Mary, dressed in embroidered satin, and loaded about the neck with innumerable strings of the largest pearls. Her waist is encircled by a zone heavy with brilliants and diamonds, and her brows surmounted by a crown of purest gold, studded with enormous emeralds.

The ceiling is arched and lofty, and the choir curious for its elaborate carving and moulded wood-work. The walls and recesses are hung with pictures from the most eminent Spanish and Italian masters; with one from a native artist, of St. Peter, made of different woods, so skilfully inlaid, as at the distance of a few feet to defy its detection from a painting in oil.

Passing out from this miracle of splendour and wealth, we retraced our steps to prison, as foul and loathsome a one as ever opened to receive the victims of misfortune. A woman with her head and face enveloped in a tattered reboso, swinging a wooden rosary and crucifix from her hand, stood under the sombre doorway as we entered, waiting for some form to be gotten through, preliminary to her incarceration. Her only companion, a sobbing boy (her son perhaps), stood by her, holding a bundle of clothes and *cesta* of fruit, her penurious store of prison comforts. Both were sheltered in the deepest shadows of the arch, the woman in an attitude of shame and sorrow, and the boy moaning most piteously, and setting down his burden at short intervals to dry his dripping cheeks with the sleeve of his jacket. A priest came out, looked on the pair, whispered with the sentinel, crossed himself, took snuff, and went on. The grated door of the prison presently opened again, and the woman, lifting her attendant in her arms, kissed him frantically over and over again, and disengaging his hands from her dress, followed the officer with her bundles up an interior flight of stairs. *Incesto*, said the sentinel, in reply to our inquiry of the crime with which she stood charged.

The city wore the stillness and quiet of death, as we traversed its streets next morning towards the eastern outlet. Every window, door, and courtyard gate, had the barred security of so many castle wickets, and in a solitary manufactory we passed were the only visible signs we met of stirring life.

Puebla is in advance of every city of Mexico, in the extent and skill of her manufacturing industry. She has more than a third of the whole spindles in the country in operation within her limits, besides considerable manufactories of woollen, paper, leather, earthenware, and glass. The vacillating government alternately stimulating these branches of enterprise by prohibitory duties on all articles conflicting with their production, and again withdrawing their bounties, or neutralizing their production, by selling permits to foreign merchants for the free importation of such articles, (to raise money on emergencies), has so deranged the value of these establishments, as not only to cause many of them to be abandoned, but to check the cultivation of wool and cotton in a material degree.

The unblushing audacity too, with which the contraband trade is maintained on the Pacific coast, and hourly enlarging on the Rio Bravo, contribute to depress the value of home commodities, and flood the country with foreign fabrics, too cheap to be competed with. Within a year or two past a more permanent tariff and rigid enforcement of the revenue laws, together with the prohibition of the raw material, have led to numerous investments of capital and labour in plantations and factories. The entire cotton crop of the republic has never reached to one hundred thousand bales, a considerable deficit under the amount required at present for home consumption. Good water-power is every where to be procured, and is in general use; the scarcity of fuel, and difficulty of its transportation, rendering steam too costly for application.

A large portion of their woollen and cotton yarns are woven by handlooms into mantas and rebosos, which find a ready and profitable sale amongst the poor and labouring classes. Coarse cloths, blankets, and baizes, are manufactured and consumed in immense quantities; and the serapes of a richer and more beautiful texture, so prized and worn for comfort and ornament by all who can afford them, command ready sale, at from fifty to six hundred dollars a-piece.

Chapter XVIII

*Route between Puebla and Perote ·
The castle of Perote · Bexar prisoners ·
Our treatment · Arrival of Santa Anna ·
Hopes of liberation · Refuse to work · How compelled ·
Sweeping the castle · Carrying sand · Epidemic
amongst prisoners · Hospital.*

The distance from Puebla to Perote is ninety-six English miles, and the country over which the road passes a wild moorland plain, intersected by mountains, whose narrow valleys are fertile and beautifully improved. Miserable villages, built of adobes, here and there chequer the roadside, which but for their contiguity to the great national highway, would long since have been deserted and abandoned to decay. Much of the surrounding soil is sandy, and the surface and shrubbery covered with a light powdered dust, which when moved by the wind, is a memorable annoyance to all who have experienced it.

It was the evening of the 21st of September, (and fifth day of our march,) before turning off through a straggling village of the same name, we reached the noted fortress of Perote, about a mile to the northwest of the town. It lies to the left of the road from the capital to Vera Cruz, and rising from out the bosom of a level plain, is visible at some distance in every direction but the east. Here it is confronted by a range of mountains, two miles distant, whose precipitous sides are inaccessible to any thing but goats, and from which water is conducted by subterraneous pipes to the castle. This formidable keep is built of stone, quadrangular in form, and having projecting horns running out at each angle one hundred and fifty feet long, and about sixty broad. It embraces an area of twenty-six acres of ground, surrounded by walls thirty feet high, being fourteen feet thick at the base, and ten at the top. The walls again are enclosed by a moat, sixty feet wide and ten deep, crossed by a drawbridge to the east connecting with a ponderous gate, the only entrance or out-let whatever to the castle. A range of prison cells, eighteen by thirty feet in depth, and surrounded by an inclined terrace reaching to within six feet of the top, runs round the entire circuit of the inter-ior walls. These cells are lofty and arched, being lighted by grated windows above massive wooden doors, and floored with tough ce-ment, ten inches deep.

The centre of the enclosure is occupied by a double square court, an acre in extent, surrounded by tiers of two-story buildings, the upper stories of three sides of the inner tier being used as officers' quarters, whilst the western side contains the chapel and governor's quarters. The lower or basement stories are occupied as barracks, and the exterior buildings used variously as work-shops, store-rooms, armories, granaries, and stables. In the northeastern and southwestern horns, are the powder magazines, the other two being appropriated at the time as lumber-houses.

Sixty-four pieces of ordnance, of nine and six pound calibre, were mounted on the terraces above the prison cells, and some brass pieces of large and small dimensions, with several howitzers, lying about the castle.

Two companies of infantry and one of artillery, comprise the or-dinary guard of the place, though a garrison of ten thousand men would scarce suffice to man it against a vigorous investment. Built during the regency of the last viceroy, it is said to have consumed five years in completion, and greatly over ten millions of dollars in cost.

Small towns are erected at the extreme points of each horn of the wall, where sentries on duty night and day, communicate the ap-proach of persons outside, by means of bells swung within. Our ar-rival being announced with a clanging alarum, and a chorus of alertas, we entered, were examined, counted, receipted for, and marched off, and soon safe under lock and key.

Whilst waiting in front of the guard-room for the despatch of these formulas, we were joined by the remnant of our unfortunate countrymen brought off from Bexar by General Woll. The sad countenances and wasted appearance of these men, but too well at-tested the sufferings of their long imprisonment. Forty-three in number, they had been here for nine weary months, the rest of their companions being dead, liberated, or escaped. Few and melancholy were our greetings, it being evident on both sides there was little solace to be imparted or received.

With the bare floors of our cells for couches, and not a blanket to the tenth man to defend us against the chilly night-winds that penetrated the gratings of our dungeons, we were left locked up and unlooked after until the next morning at nine o'clock, when we received a welcome breakfast of coffee and good bread, and were told we could enjoy the freedom of the prison until 3 P. M. At noon we were again regaled with a good dinner, and being rested, refreshed, and distributed in rooms where we were not too crowded, matters began to assume a more agreeable aspect than they wore upon our entrance.

Captain Bradley, one of the Bexar captives, received his release during the day, and his transports of happiness, at being liberated, diffused a sympathy of joy throughout the whole prison. Squalid, penniless, and without a friend outside from whom he could hope to receive relief, he scarce stayed to bid us adieu, so impatient was he to answer the summons of home and freedom.

On the fifth day of our confinement we received a visit from General Jose Maria Jarea, governor or commandant of the fortress, who, after a personal inspection of our quarters, and benevolent inquiry into the character of our entertainment and wardrobes, left us with the assurances that every humanity should be extended us, even to a needful supply of shoes, and mats to sleep upon. He was a fine martial-looking old fellow, with such a monomania for personal cleanliness, as to suggest the propriety of our taking to the moat next day, and performing a long suspended ablution of our persons. As such a proposition was mutually gratifying, we honoured the governor's invitation by a general acceptance. With a competent guard, next day we adjourned outside the walls in a body, and underwent a thorough cleansing, the governor meanwhile looking down upon us from the parapet above, seemingly as intent upon our purification as though he destined us for an immediate levee.

On the evening of the 7th of October, General Santa Anna arrived and took lodgings at the castle, on his way to Manga de Clavo. It was twilight when his guard and *coche* came clattering over the drawbridge, amid a salute of twenty-one guns and an incessant din from the sentry-bells. By dawn the following morning he was off again, making it a point, invariably, to adapt his movements, whether pressed for time or not, to that courier-like celerity characteristic of his great model.

On the 13th, letters, with their seals broken, were handed us from our comrades in the capital, who had been kept behind sick, announcing the deaths of two of their number, Mr. Irwin and O. R. Willis. The old governor shortly after joined us, with the welcome intelligence that we would all be liberated in twenty days, and his intimation was swallowed *sine grano*, not a doubt being entertained but it was derived from the president himself, on his recent visit.

A number of Mexican convicts, who were confined in the castle, and had heretofore been employed in sweeping and watering it, left on the 19th, and orders were issued the same evening that we should assume their degrading task on the following day. This we peremptorily informed the officer who brought the command we would not do, and referred him indignantly to our rights under the capitulation at Mier, solemnly agreed upon and reduced to writing. He shook his head when informed of the grounds of our protest, and referring to our submission at Tacubaya, very frankly declared, if we held out against the order, similar severities would be adopted to enforce our acquiescence. We attempted to weaken the force of the fatal precedent by an argument based on the atrocity of compelling our obedience to an unjust and unrighteous requirement, but finding the man deaf to our metaphysics, we next insisted upon the superior respectability of turnpiking over the vile offices now threatened to be imposed on us. After hearing us out in our logical remonstrance, he replied, with provoking coolness, that we would be honoured with the most respectable labour that was to do; but in the meanwhile advised us to offer no opposition to the inevitable necessity of obedience to the castle discipline, and, with this friendly injunction, we separated.

At nine o'clock next morning, the usual hour for the meal, no breakfast was brought us; but the same officer appeared, and politely requested to be informed whether we had resolved to comply with the commands of the previous evening. We firmly repeated our protest, and, without a word in reply, he gave some directions to the sergeant on duty, and retired. Every morning since our residence in the prison, we had been permitted to leave our cells and stroll about the streets of the castle till the afternoon, enjoying such recreations as were admissible under the rules of the establishment. This morning, as soon as the officer had departed, the doors of our apartments were relocked, and several hours elapsed before our solitude was intruded on. At the expiration of this time the doors were again opened, and some of our men, who were carpenters by trade, called out, and the residue fastened in.

The hour of dinner came and passed off without the usual visit from our commissary. The day was beautiful outside, the sunbeams clustering upon the grated window in such tempting and genial warmth, as made the cold and dreary shadows of our cells doubly comfortless. We had made repeated and clamorous applications for water during the day, which were as little heeded as were the mute appeals of our empty stomachs. Some of our merrier comrades, by way of manifesting their indifference to the neglect we were enduring, sung and danced so very boisterously as excited fears of bringing down the immediate vengeance of the officer of the day. Still the evening wore on, and neither punishment nor reproof, food, water, nor inquiries followed its decline. Disappointed in their efforts to provoke a visit from the police, and exhausted with their exercises, our gleemakers ceased their quavers and saltations, and sunk upon the floor as spiritless and moody as the rest. Darkness set in, and with it came an increase of hunger, cold, and thirst. Our jokers tried their best drollery and raciest humour, without so much as a smile of acknowledgement from their most susceptible admirers. Several who had been noisily vociferous for drink and nourishment during the day, now crouched in a corner of the apartment relapsed into gloomy silence, save the busy churning of their teeth as aguish chills came over them. They ventured at length upon the hint that sweeping was no great labour at last, and work was work, call it by what name you would, and that for their part they were agreed to do the dusting, provided the rest would consent. No applause or dissent whatever accompanying their proposition, silence resumed its empire in the cell, and by midnight all succeeded in getting asleep.

Such marvellous dreams as were related next morning of broomsticks, would have bewildered a conclave of witches. By a singular coincidence, gentlemen wholly unaccustomed to these nocturnal partings of soul and body, were conscious of their immortal spirits having gone out to dinners where the sirloin was stuck full of broomstraws, and steaming covers being removed, revealed in place of capons and calves-heads, nothing but the manifold varieties of the detested article. Some had approached crystal fountains of delicious water, pouring like melted silver down the mountain-side, when, all at once, there sprung up in their place magical forests of broom-corn, that utterly obscured all view of the beverage. The aguish had been enticed to thaw their frozen limbs by blazing fires, which, when approached, were extinguished by weird women, sweeping them out with great bell-shaped street-dusters, on which they had been riding. Others, whilst cleaning a distant part of the castle, found an aperture concealed from view by the filth they removed, disclosing a passage out, through which we might all escape from confinement. It required no Daniel to interpret these visions, as they all clearly portended the increasing popularity of the governor's proposition.

Hungry as a herd of wolves, and as thirsty as newly awakened topers, we crowded around the door at ten o'clock as the key turned in the heavy wards of the lock. A limited supply of bread and water was brought in, and whilst diligently engaged upon these, the governor's ambassador entered. With the usual suavity of tone and manner, he again desired to know what result our deliberations had led to, touching his orders. Seeing we were not to be starved outright, and vainly imagining the speedy arrival of a second course of refreshments, some of the sturdiest of our fellows promptly reaffirmed their determination not to sweep. Others, and a majority, expressed a sullen assent to the requirements, on condition of being immediately supplied with necessary provisions and chamber furniture. This the officer either did not understand or chose to misconceive, as but a few minutes elapsed after his departure, before a smith with a file of soldiers brought in a load of chains, and began fettering us without the slightest distinction of persons or opinions.

Having concluded the operation, we were left to reflect at our leisure upon the evils incident to such disunited counsels as afflicted us. Famine, though a rude and dogmatical reasoner, rarely fails of achieving the persuasion she proposes. By five o'clock, we succeeded in obtaining an interview with the governor's diplomat, when a brief parley served to adjust our little misconceptions, and a steaming joint, and profusion of other delicacies, promptly placed at our disposal by the magnanimous victor, served to rob our subjection of its sting.

There was no procrastination on the part of the enemy in gathering the fruits of his victory, and an early hour on the following day, found the castle enveloped in a cloud of dust, from our indefatigable brooms! The governor's quarters came in for more than their rightful share of these interesting proofs of our diligence; windows, doors, and walls being assailed by such furious columns of powder, as to bring the old gentleman in person to the spot, to counter-march us to a more distant scene of operation.

Those whose task it was to remove in barrows the collected piles of filth, were extremely indignant with their occupation, but the sweepers grew to relish their branch of business so well as to repine at the prospect of its speedy termination. The superintendents set over us were tolerably clothed with ashes if they were not in sack-cloth, and, though frequently relieved, not an officer or subaltern could at last be found, who would venture inside the canopy of dust, under which we plied our furious task.

Two days we prosecuted this pleasing vengeance, when, at the close of the second, our tools were taken away, and the whole gar-rison turned out the next morning, that their quarters might be cleaned of the defilement that had penetrated them.

After acquitting ourselves so well in this first undertaking, no marvel that our task-masters should be eager to find us in further employment. This was soon contrived in setting us to pack sand in hand-barrows, from near a mile outside, into the castle, to repair various portions of the fortifications that were going to decay. In this occupation we were securely guarded, little opportunity being offered us, either of neglecting our labour or getting away. Our loads were heavy, and our chains, which no entreaty could induce them to remove, galled our ankles, until the men boldly cut them loose and threw them from their cells into the streets. This offence car-ried many to the calaboose, and supplied others with double irons, in which they were still compelled to work.

An epidemic broke out amongst the prisoners about this time, and there being no suitable hospital provided at the castle, the sick were sent to the town, where a proper building was appropriated for their reception. Here they were well cared for, the physicians and nurses being attentive, and every thing appropriate of necessity or comfort being provided them.

Chapter XIX

St. Carlos day · Its celebration in the
castle · Devotion of two Catholic Texans ·
Rage of an epidemic amongst the prisoners ·
Rumours concerning it · Proclamation of Santa Anna
and the governor · Sanitary regulations · Storms in the
valley · Christmas · Monotony of our confinement ·
Cessation of epidemic · The 1st of March ·
Release of Ogden and thirteen of our men
in Mexico · Visit from the American
minister · His communications
to us.

November the 4th being St. Carlos day, it was celebrated with all
the pomp and splendour possible, in the castle. Several previous
days had been employed by every member of the garrison, in making
preparations for the joyful occasion; and bonfires, illuminations,
rockets, streamers, and devices, were made to contribute their various aids in doing honour to the holy patron of the occasion. Every
part of the castle was adorned, mass celebrated in the chapel morning and evening, officers and soldiers tricked out in their gayest apparel, and the prisoners presented with a new suit of striped regimentals, which they were requested to put on, and unite in the
festivities.

A full-length figure of St. Carlos about three feet in height, (a
jolly-looking old gentleman,) dressed in a full suit of canonicals, and
carried on the shoulders of four sacristans, was made to perform the
circuit of the castle, followed by his reverence the priest, at the head
of a numerous procession of soldiers, prisoners, and convicts. Two
of our fellows, who had become converts to Romanism on the road
up to Mexico, but had soon after relapsed into their habitual neutrality towards all creeds and rituals, thought the present a con-

163

zens of Perote, (many of whom perished with it,) whilst it confuted the decision of our leeches, puzzled the Mexican faculty what to determine it. A violent headache, accompanied by fever and immediate general prostration of the system, followed up in a few hours by delirium, were its general symptoms. So sudden was the attack, and so rapid and agonizing the stages, that suspicions began to gain ground even in the capital, that foul play had been used on us, and poison employed to complete what the musket had spared.

Santa Anna, informed of these rumours, manifested the deepest sensibility to them, despatching an express to the castle, urging on the governor every expedient he could devise to arrest its progress. At his urgent solicitation and command, our physicians were united with the medical staff of the castle and town in post mortem examinations of such as had died, and their inquest, accompanied by certificates of the general discipline of the prison remitted to him.

Amongst the many diverting sanitary regulations promulgated by the governor and his medical advisers, not the least amusing was one interdicting us from the use of water before 12 A. M., either for washing or drinking. In lieu of this Washingtonian beverage, we were supplied every morning with abundance of excellent coffee, and, for some days, homœopathic doses of brandy, that materially tended to recommend our change of regimen. *Chili* and nourishing soups were also added to the catalogue of our diet; so that all were prone to be friends with the epidemic, so long as it refrained to fasten directly upon themselves.

No intermission of labour was allowed such as were well, and notwithstanding their great anxiety to check the disease at the earliest period of its appearance, the most decided premonitories were required precedent to sending the patient to the hospital. Our chains, too, were in no instance dispensed with, unless in case of illness; and, from repeated searches of our persons and rooms, the stock of instruments for removing them at night became so alarmingly diminished, that we resolved to wear them patiently, sooner than provoke the loss of things so indispensable to our future escape.

The weather in this valley, since the 1st of November, continued cold and chilly, rain falling, with very few exceptions, every day. The thunder-storms that occur here are the most magnificent and sublime conceivable. Enormous masses of clouds, drifting up from the coast, with racehorse speed, and piling themselves bank on bank, from the lowest mountain spurs, up and around the peaks of

Orizaba, Tepiacualca, and the Coffre of Perote, at one moment blazing with brilliant lightning along the uttermost wings of the horizon, revealing the ragged sides of the dark *barrancas*, and the next waking every recess with bellowing thunder, whilst floods and flying mists dashed down upon the plains, were spectacles of frequent grandeur that not even walls and cells could shut out from us.

Christmas came, and with it the reminiscence of a tedious year's captivity, without one ray of hope to illumine the next that was to follow. This anniversary of our bloody struggle at Mier was too fresh in the minds of our jailers to admit us to a participation in the holy ceremonies with which themselves celebrated it. We were accordingly left to drape it in the most dramatic hues of memory we could in our solitary dungeons. The following day being that of our surrender, we were let out, an indulgence we were at a loss to account for, as no display of triumph whatever was permitted to insult us by a reference to our disastrous capitulation.

The month of January wore off in dull and monotonous confinement, relieved by such occasional toil as the elements without allowed us. A callous insensibility to the present, and gloomy despair of the future, seemed hourly stealing upon every heart, and the poetic fiction of being friends with our chains, promised, at no distant time, to be literally realized. Our very speculations grew as old and trite as our reminiscences, and the latest criticism on the governor's daughter, the castle's strength, or the officers' habits, was received with such yawns as time out of mind have strangled the thrice-told tale. The jest and song were utterly obsolete; puns and conundrums as hazardous as treason, and the most distant allusions to home or friends deprecated as heartless and insolent levity. One only theme was ever green, racy, and exhaustless, and that was vengeance, in some form, most direful upon our oppressors. Our numbers, amounting to but a few above a hundred and fifty, and these separated by sickness, divided during day by different occupations, and lodged at night in separate cells, rendered any plan for a general rising hopeless, from the country, as from the castle, not a solitary relaxation occurring in the lynx-eyed vigilance with which we were watched, sleeping or waking. There were times when the desperate talked of the magazine, and one common destruction; but this, beside its impracticability of being reached, was known to contain but a slender stock of powder, and too remote from the occupied parts of the castle to effect the destruction meditated.

February came and went, with little beyond its storms and cold to vary the usual routine of our prison life. The epidemic ceased towards the close of the month, and the invalids returned from the town to the castle, to render up their languid and emaciated frames to other and less enviable sufferings.

Their incipient convalescence (they told us), was devoted to various plans of escape from the hospital, but such was the fidelity of their guards, (without whose connivance all attempts were hopeless,) that their proposals were denounced, and a stricter watch kept over them until they were able to be removed. The fear of Santa Anna's vengeance predominates in the minds of his soldiers over every instinct of humanity or avarice.

The 1st of March we could not fail to observe an unusual demeanour on the part of the Mexican officers towards us. Their commands heretofore issued in mild and courteous tones were suddenly substituted by harsh and peremptory mandates, accompanied by oaths and angry expressions of look and manner. Whilst receiving our rations at noon, we were farther surprised by discovering a piece of artillery drawn up at the northern terminus of the street, and so directed as to range the avenue on which our cells were situated. Additional sentries were every where on duty, and as soon as our dinner was through with, we were ordered into our rooms and locked up. At dark, a line of patrols were stationed outside, whose hails were repeated at frequent intervals through the night, and when morning came, we could see the whole garrison drawn up and under arms. These formidable precautions were soon after explained by the governor in person, who, after dismissing his array, came to inform us how vigilant he was, and how futile and fatal would be any renewal of the attempt to rise upon our guard. It was with difficulty we prevailed on the old gentleman to believe he had been made the victim of an idle hoax, nor did his fears and superfluous vigilance subside for some time after.

On the 3d instant, Mr. Ogden, a Mier prisoner, received his liberty and passport, and on the 4th, thirteen of our companions who had been left in Mexico reached the town of Perote on their way to Vera Cruz. On the 11th, General Waddy Thompson, the American Minister, made us a visit on his road to the United States. He expressed the deepest sympathy in our misfortunes, but beside confirming the reported armistice between Mexico and Texas, could furnish us with no other information in regard to our destinies. No provision in reference to us had been so much as alluded to in the armistice, and no efforts that he was apprised of, open or secret, were making by our country for the amelioration of our lot. Deserted and abandoned by those to whom alone we were entitled to look for sympathy and succour, our fortitude did not desert us, but, nerved for the worst, we thanked the generous American for his successful exertions in behalf of our more fortunate comrades, and bade him adieu.

Chapter XX

Release of the Bexar prisoners ·
Remarks upon their treatment · Escape
of sixteen prisoners · Confusion of the garrison
and rage of the governor · Mode of escape · Committee
of safety and vigilance · Letter from General Jackson ·
Santa Anna's lady · Letter from General Green · Sham
fight and participation of prisoners · Recapture of
seven of the fugitives · Depositions · Adornment
of the castle · Release of the author.

On the 23d of March, an order was received from the government directing the release of the Bexar prisoners. This clemency was the fruit of the assiduous importunity of General Waddy Thompson, whose zealous and untiring efforts for the liberation of a hapless and unrecognised body of captives, entitle him to the highest meed of enlightened philanthropy.

An unoffending and peaceable class of citizens, engaged in the prosecution of civil and domestic pursuits, they had been surprised in their distant homes by a cowardly and marauding banditti, and torn from their families and fireside-altars to grace the triumph of their craven captor. Since then they had been detained by the dictator in his dungeons for sixteen months, without other warrant than his own wanton love of tyranny and inhumanity. For every pound of fetters we wore, a Mexican soldier's life had already atoned. But no widow or orphan's wail appealed to the vengeance of their country against a solitary individual of this unfortunate corps. They had scarcely resisted when assailed, been submissive and subordinate on their march, and during their imprisonment, and yet had been made to endure enormities which the pen recoils from inditing. Our greatest charge against the tyrant, was his sanction of the vile perfidy of his subaltern Ampudia, in violating the solemn stipulations of the surrender. This was a contempt of all the laws of chivalry and civilized war, only worthy of the Mexican nation and their dishonoured chief. But we had ravaged his territory, pillaged his towns, and butchered his soldiery sent to expel us. There was a degraded but still a human motive for his severity towards us. In the other case there was no justification in reason, humanity, or revenge itself, for his barbarous retention and oppression of these men. None was ever pretended to be plead, and none can be produced but from the punic code of Mexican policy.

Before receiving their passports, the conditions of their release required from them an oath they would not again bear arms in the contest between Texas and Mexico. This form being observed, they were ordered to pack up their little mockery of baggage, and after a mournful and tearful leave of us, turned out upon the plains to find their way back to their desolate homes as they could best contrive. Van Ness, who had been a Santa Fe prisoner, was detained a fortnight later; and at the end of that time received his credentials and departed.

On the morning of the 26th, the castle was the scene of one of the most amusing and fantastic hubbubs ever witnessed inside its venerable precincts.

On opening one of the cells in which the prisoners were confined, it was discovered that sixteen out of the twenty-seven inmates were missing. The astonished turnkey, who had securely locked them in on the previous evening, instantly discovered the enormous reduction of his charge, and in answer to his breathless inquiries of their whereabouts, was pointed to a huge hole in the corner, some two feet in diameter, and of incomprehensible depth and direction. Stunned with amazement and apprehension, he could only stare down the gloomy labyrinth for a time, then bounded out of the door, shouting at the top of his voice as he ran towards the governor, "Los Tejanos han salido!—Los Tejanos estan bajo el castillo!—Los Tejanos han escapado!" In a minute the bells were clattering away in their turrets with a fury that threatened to bring them to the ground; the cry to arms was heard from a hundred voices—the drums beat to quarters—and the whole garrison were forming—most of the officers (and the commandant amongst them) rushing to their posts in a dishabille we decline to particularize. For near twenty minutes this scene of martial preparation was going on for a rencontre with a foe, whose mysterious invisibility rendered him tenfold more dreaded. At length the commandant, having obtained some clue to the monstrous occurrence, marched boldly up at the head of about fifty men with their muskets cocked and at a charge, and forming them carefully in front of the open cells, entered brandishing his drawn sword amongst the survivors of the *escapada*. These poor fellows, thinking their doom was sealed and their executioners ready, were ranged against the farthermost wall of their dungeon, silently and dejectedly awaiting their fate.

Halting near the threshold, and regarding the immovable forms before him with mingled rage and suspicion, the old man demanded where and how their companions were concealed. With their eyes fixed on the soldiers outside, the interrogator had thrice to repeat his inquiry before the abstracted Texans deigned him a reply. Nodding to the gaping aperture, which was barely visible from where the governor stood, they left the sequel to his sympathetic imagination. Slowly approaching it, and scrutinizing the features of his informants as he advanced as distrustful of some stratagem, he peered into the abyss, and all farther doubts were at once solved.

The hole which had been cut through the cement floor of the cell, penetrated the earth perpendicularly down. An officer being despatched outside, discovered after a long search its *debouchure* ascending through the reeds of the moat, which on that side of the castle was kept free of water for purposes of health and preservation of the wall. The foundation was estimated to reach some four feet below the bottom of the moat, and our men were compelled from its immense thickness to undermine it. They had been engaged about six weeks in the enterprise, working at night, and hiding the loose earth as they dug it under the platform of boards on which they slept; and this so secretly and securely that most of their roommates protest in the most solemn manner to the present hour their ignorance of the affair until the morning after their escape.

It is impossible to depict the rage and distress of the commandant, when made sensible, by the descent of one of his men, that the fugitives were not concealed in the hole, but actually outside and away. He by turns stormed, raved, threatened, and wept. Having despatched various parties, mounted and on foot, in pursuit, he retired to the cell to vent his displeasure on the remainder of its inmates. These he denounced alternately as scoundrels and fools; the former, that they concealed and aided the toils of their companions, and the latter, because they had not acted like men of sense and fled also. The unhappy subjects of his rage stoutly denied his first accusation, but covertly plead guilty to the last. In the first ebullition of his wrath he ordered every prisoner (but the carpenters engaged in his workshops) to be chained in pairs, threatening the hapless accomplices of those who had fled with speedy and inevitable death. The officers who had charge of our cells were instantly arrested and confined, and the utmost vengeance of the Dictator denounced against them. In his paroxysms of lamentation he several times alluded to the penalties that would attach to him personally, involving a certain loss of rank and command, and possibly a more capital infliction. Some ten days after, the old gentleman affected to have received a despatch from Santa Anna, amongst whose other contents he asserted was a statement from the Dictator, that the arrival of the news of this transaction found him with a signed and sealed order for our general release in his hands, which was forthwith used to light his cigarrito. We had too often been gulled with such half-formed intentions respecting us, to place any confidence in the governor's statement, knowing Santa Anna was not fain to be governed by such capricious pretexts in cases like our own.

The new committee of safety who succeeded to the custody of us, (comprising some of the most experienced officers and subalterns of the garrison,) maintained a diligent and lynx-eyed scrutiny of our persons and cells, that destroyed all further hopes of another successful burrow. Morning and evening, this solemn delegation, armed with sticks, swords, and bayonets, visited our quarters, and, after a Bow Street examination of our persons, proceeded to search every cranny and fissure in the walls and floor, sounding and picking the whole surface of the cells, as though they were supposed to contain as many secret passages and traps as a feudal stronghold. In these examinations, several of our fellows who had managed to win upon their confidence, affected to assist, pointing out little crevices they had themselves scratched, and producing lumps of earth they brought from without, as proofs of further plots against the repair of the fortress.

Sunday's mail, of April the 7th, brought us the copy of a letter, said to be on its way to Santa Anna from General Andrew Jackson, interposing in our behalf. An application from so distinguished and virtuous a quarter revived new hopes in our almost callous hearts, and cheered the despondent with something near an assurance of freedom. But for General Jackson, Santa Anna would now have been sleeping at the foot of a Texan gibbet, or sweating under the drudgery to which a more untoward fate had consigned the victims of his policy.

The 20th being the saint's day of the president's lady, largesses of money, and little comforts, were distributed through the castle, amongst the soldiers and prisoners. Those bestowed upon the prisoners, we considered very *personal* in their character, being three cents' worth of soap to the man, with the privilege of immediately using it in renovating our complexions in the moat. All distinguished families in Mexico have their tutelary saints, to whom a shrine is erected in their mansions, and their festivals kept, with an elegance and magnificence proportioned to the resources of the devotee. Strong rivalries are thus excited between the especial worshippers of the different *santos* of the calendar, and presents and alms liberally distributed, to obtain *éclat* for their anniversaries. The Lady Santa Anna, by universal testimony, deserved herself to be canonised, being renowned for all the virtues and humanities that adorn the most chaste and elevated standards of female worth. Over the relentless selfishness of her husband, she is reported to have enjoyed no ordinary supremacy, mitigating the rigour of his resentments, and saving him from the commission of numberless atrocities, by the influence of her benevolent counsels. She is recently dead, embalmed in the affectionate regrets of the Mexican people, and consecrated in the esteem and gratitude of all the unfortunate whom her tireless charities have aided and relieved.

A letter from General Thomas Green, (who had escaped from Perote previous to our arrival, and reached home in safety,) advised us that the Texan Congress had appropriated funds for our relief, which had been remitted at the date of his communication. Had they ever reached their destination, they would materially have contributed to lighten our sufferings, as many suffered from want of the most common articles of dress appropriate to the season. Though they never arrived, there was something consolatory in the assurance conveyed that we were not forgotten and abandoned by our countrymen.

On the evening of the 27th, we were permitted to witness from behind the pickets of the moat, a grand review of the garrison, concluded with a sham attack on the castle from a party outside. The feints, advances, retreats, and sorties, were managed pretty much as usual, and without any important loss or advantage on either side. Being so situated as to be debarred from uniting in the assault on the castle, we turned our puissant arms in its defence, and aided no little in repelling the assailants with showers of clods, whenever they approached within reach. Being encouraged by the old governor from the wall, in this voluntary and unexpected co-operation with his forces, we took occasion to disperse a forlorn hope, who were nearing an imaginary breach in the wall, by knocking down a corporal and private, with pebbles we obtained from the ditch. This unexpected charge produced an immediate cessation of hostilities, and our enraged commandant displayed his Mexican gratitude, by withdrawing us from the field, and threatening us all with the calaboose. Our slingers were in chains, or the enemy's loss would have proved much more serious.

By the 1st of May, seven of the sixteen prisoners who had escaped were retaken and brought back to the castle. They had left at nine o'clock P. M., and parting outside in squads of two and three, pursued different directions. Some started for Tampico; some down the highway, to overtake the Bexar prisoners, who had been liberated at Perote; others returned to Pueblo, and the capital itself. These latter were enabled, by going directly to the least-suspected places, to lie concealed until the first fury of pursuit had spent itself, when procuring passports, disguises, and money, from friendly sources, they left the country without challenge.

The depositions of those recaptured were taken immediately on their arrival at the castle. Upon being sworn, they revealed all the circumstances attending their break, deposing explicitly to having been employed six weeks in the operation of cutting out. These statements, instead of being recorded by the secretary as they were delivered and interpreted, were entered upon his minutes so as to make the time occupied in cutting the hole three days, in place of the number of weeks they had confessed to. This perversion of testimony being adopted to secure from responsibility the officers under arrest for neglect of duty. By such barefaced perjury and forgery of clerk and commission, did the tyrant's slaves elude his resentment.

Santa Anna had long been expected at Perote from his estate, on his way to the capital. Every preparation that could flatter his vanity (from such a source) had been studiously made by the governor and garrison for his reception. Our labours in repairing and beautifying the fortress with paint, paving, and whitewash, had been stimulated by every incentive they dared offer us, and early in May the whole was completed. The soiled and blackened walls of the old building glistened with the hues of the new-fallen snow; the court of the central square was paved with cement, and coloured the deepest crimson; crumbling masonry was reset, broken doors renewed, verandahs repainted, and all things put in trimmest array for the expected visit.

The 16th of May brought an order for the author's release, which release was as unexpected to me as it was mysterious to all the prisoners within the walls of this hateful place. No hint of an application having been made in my favour was ever named, nor did I know that my friends were using any exertions to procure my liberty. And after a painful parting with the comrades whose varied and mutual fortunes he has thus far feebly traced, he left the castle and took quarters for the night in the neighbouring town of Perote.

As the remainder of this narrative will embrace his personal adventures and observations in Mexico, an appropriate change of style will be adopted in their relation.

Chapter XXI

*Return to Mexico · Changes since the
conquest · The lakes · Architecture · Dress
of the upper classes · Mexican lady · Her Donzella ·
Castes · Creoles · Negroes and Indians ·
Character, condition, and employment
of the latter.*

Something more than ten days had elapsed since my liberation from
Perote, when I found myself comfortably installed in the house of a
friend, a short distance removed from the great plaza of the capital.
I had reached the city by the usual route from the east, after a fatigu-
ing journey, through which the squalor of my apparel and appearance were ample protection against any annoyances of travel but
those which are every where incident to a tattered garb and slender
purse.

The country over which I had previously been driven an abject
captive at the point of the bayonet, I now trod with the leisure of a
lord, and the buoyant heart of newborn freedom. And who that has
ever seen the morning smile, the noontide sleep, or the sunset glory
of a Mexican May, need be told the magical loveliness in which
earth, air, and sky looms at such a season. The vast and dreary tor-
por of its desert mountains, the music of their silver streamlets, the
wild retreats of their dark banditti, the gemmed beauty and fragrant
breath of the flowered plains, the lakes of tremulous crystal, dimp-
ling under the dropping dew of tall flowers, whose opened chalices
of gold and silver margin their shores, and over all its clear, vapourless, and unflecked skies, glistening in pensive light and loveliness,
as soft as

Future joys to fancy's eye.

Over charms like these and numerous others, whose glowing enchantment defy delineation, the step of the traveller is wooed and

detained at every advance towards the proud and picturesque metropolis. Though toiling near it for months, imprisoned within its outskirts, and circuiting its suburbs on two occasions, I was now for the first time inside its majestic maze of palaces and temples.

Three centuries have elapsed since this magnificent valley (near one hundred and fifty miles in circumference), with its no less magnificent capital, passed from the hands of its aboriginal masters into those of their Spanish conquerors. With the fall of the empire of this interesting people, the destruction of their monuments of art and civilization have kept pace, until, between the superstition, avarice, and change of their successors, but few vestiges remain to bear witness to their ancient refinement and enterprise. The visiter who looks to find the modern city the same lake-born Tenochtitlan of olden time, perched in the centre of inland seas, and accessible from the surrounding continent by great dikes and causeways, or streeted with canals whose sluggish waters are traversed by gondolas and bucentaurs, will be far from realizing his antique dreams of the Montezumas' Venice. When the last of this confiding and doomed line of monarchs stood upon the summit of his great temple, and displayed to the greedy eyes of the pirate Cortes, the splendour of his city and the surrounding creations, its canals and aqueducts, its groves and floating gardens, its pictorial palaces and barbaric shrines, it was a higher specimen of gorgeous architecture and poetic landscape than the Spanish substitute that now occupies its site.

Its subjugation and pillage was followed by a Vandal destruction, that aimed to obliterate every landmark of its former features from the memory of contemporaneous generations, or the rescue of succeeding ones. The priest and the soldier vied with each other in the work of desolation, and what was spared by the ferocity of the one was devoted by the bigotry of the other. Its houses were levelled as its conquest advanced, the torch was applied to the palace and temple, when their sack was completed, and the remaining ruins that neither powder nor flame could consume, flung into the lakes and canals to choke and destroy them.

The adjacent lakes of Chalco and Tezcuco, Zumpango and San Christoval, once the flowery and bubbling vases of its mountain streams, above whose affluent depths armed brigantines rode, though still remaining, are drained and shrunken, until their midst are but pools for the wading fisherman, and their shores marshy coverts for wild-fowl.

The levels of these lakes are many feet above that of the city, over which they were wont at distant periods to pour their swollen waters, in destructive inundations. A recurrence of this calamity is now provided against by a gigantic desagua (or sewer), that empties their dangerous accumulations into the river Tula, whence they are discharged without injury to the valley. Haciendas and villages, embowered in luxuriant foliage, still dot their shores, and the canals that connect them with the capital are filled from dawn till sunset with innumerable Indian skiffs, bearing their rich products to the city markets.

For its extent of splendid and massive architecture, Mexico has no rival on the continent, and is unsurpassed by any city of Europe in the beauty, regularity, and general effect of its arrangement. Its population cannot be accurately fixed at less than two hundred thousand souls, exclusive of the numbers who swarm within its gates during the day, from the towns in the vicinity. Of these, perhaps, one-fifth are *léperos*, an unclean, vicious, and miserable class of beggars, who inhabit the hovels of the outskirts, infesting every point of the city with their presence, begging, stealing, robbing, and assassinating, as hunger and opportunity may incite them. But the great mass of its edifices (aside from its palaces, convents, monasteries, cathedrals, and public offices,) are embraced in squares of uniformity, built of stone in the most solid and durable form, and painted with the gayest colours. Their dwellings are admirably adapted to the genial climate that surrounds them, having from two to three stories of height, enclosing a *patio* or square court, and adorned in front by arches and balconies filled with fruit and flower trees, whilst the whole is surmounted by the *azotea* or flat-tiled roof, crowned with bloom, the favourite resort of the family during these nights of perennial beauty and mildness. Nothing can exceed the ordinary seclusion and privacy of these residences, nor their brilliant appearance on holidays, when, flung open from pavement to terrace, they disclose throngs of lovely and richly-clad women, curtained by gorgeous tapestries of satin and velvet.

The dress of the wealthy and fashionable classes of Mexico, excel, in splendour and costliness, that of any people in the world, whose style of costume, in any degree, assimilates to their own. From the breaking out of the revolution, the popularity of the army has been so ascendant as to leave but a limited portion of the lay gentry unentitled to the use of the uniform. Generals, colonels, majors, and captains, are more common here than in the United States; and, besides, the numbers of those who have served and retired on pensions or offices, all who have ever held commissions, seem to arrogate the privilege of sporting the insignia of their former rank. Hence, uniforms, stiff with gold and embroidery, encounter you at every step, whilst the fanciful and more graceful attire of the civic elegant, frogged, laced, bedizened, and tasselled, lose nothing by comparison with their martial rivals.

Standing in her balcony, attired for the holiday, the drive, or her devotions, the Mexican lady reflects the full power of the best combination of foreign and native costume. Her *Parisien* gown, falling short in its embroidered skirts of her well-turned ankles and feet, (delicate almost to deformity,) and clothed in the invariable satin slipper and silken stockings, her rich lace mantilla, revealing a border of her raven hair, and depending in graceful folds down the voluptuous line of her rounded proportions, her ears, neck, and fingers, shining with the blaze of diamonds, and her dimpled hand clutching the pictured fan, the wand of the fair enchantress, before whose coquettish wave all hearts sink subdued, are the outlines of a style, below which the opulent and tonnish never venture abroad.

At some other portal of the house, may be seen her *donzella*, luxuriating in the freedom and fancy of the national *dishabille*. Her stinted petticoat of gaudy hue, challenges a more extended survey of her white clocked stockings and flowered slippers, whilst the moulded outline it drapes below, disdaining all restraint above the waist, smiles through a snowy chemise of worked linen cambric, like pensive lights through silver mist. Her plaited hair hangs down between her round, brown shoulders, and should she go out, a long figured shawl or *reboso* envelopes her person and features to the eyes, whose dazzling brilliance and liquid tenderness it were profane to hide.

In the streets of the capital, (as throughout the republic,) the variety of hues into which their castes run, destroys every thing like a national complexion in the people. Prior to the revolution, the *native* Spaniards, (called Chapetones,) not exceeding a hundred thousand in numbers, not only enjoyed the exclusive authority and wealth of the country, but deported themselves as beings of a superior order, openly asserting the inferiority of other classes, and denying them all honours or liberal occupations. To be *white*, was then a badge of rank, and so arrogantly was it esteemed, that Europeans and their immediate descendants styled themselves *par excellence*, the *genté de razon*, in contradistinction to all other amalgamations of race. The fall of the Spanish power was followed by the expulsion of nearly all these people from the country, and the confiscation of their property. The few who still linger are objects of perpetual jealousy, and only allowed to exist under the strictest surveillance from the government. Notwithstanding all political distinctions, founded on colour, were formally abolished by the revolution, the ancient prejudices on this head are still maintained in the establishment of social rank, and great importance attached and conceded to the nearest approach to European blood and complexion. The Creoles, who assert in this view the supremacy claimed by the Spaniards, are estimated at near a million in number, and though but the smallest portion of these are free from a mixture of Indian blood, they still form a privileged caste, with whom is lodged the civil, military, and ecclesiastical dignities of the country.

Many of them, descended from the ancient conquerors, enjoy titles and fortunes almost princely, being enriched by speculations in the mines, and enormous landed estates; from which they derive incomes adequate to the indulgence of the utmost splendour and ostentation.

Next to them in a descending scale are the Mestizoes or mixed castes, some two millions and upwards in number, made up of every admixture of the primitive colours, of Indian, negro, and white. The union of the white with the Indian constitutes the mestizo; the white and negro the mulatto; and the Indian and negro the zambo. The union of the white again with the mulatto produces the quateron; the union of the quateron and white, the quinteron; and the offspring of the white and quinteron is received and accounted as white. The negroes do not reach above a hundred thousand in number; whilst the Indians or aborigines are computed at more than four of their seven millions of population.

These last constituting the mass of the physical force of the country, are kept in a state of ignorance, slavery, and degradation, in few respects better than the slaves of the United States. Nominally entitled to political and personal freedom, and paying a considerable impost or capitation tax towards the support of the government, they are literally the hewers of wood and drawers of water for the rest of their countrymen. Oppressed and downtrodden, they are not unfrequently subjected to the lash on the estates they are employed to cultivate. Out of their enormous total of four millions, less than a hundred thousand can read or write, and, without any prospective scheme for their enlightenment or regeneration, their future weight or control in the government may be estimated by a provision of the present constitution, which denies the right of suffrage to all the uneducated after the year 1850.

For these the revolution has done nothing, or worse than nothing. The united mental degradation and religious superstition in which it found them remains unaltered; and an uninterrupted submission for centuries of slavery, seems to have rendered them indifferent to any higher aims than the gratification of their simple and lowly wants of appetite. Steeped in a Helotism of which their constitutional rights are but a cruel mockery, their lives are passed between work and sleep, with no sympathies or speculations in contests, or institutions, save those imparted them by their bigoted priesthood, or ignorant magistracy.

Their religion is of a part with their political darkness, the rites and idolatries of their ancient heathenism being strongly blent with their crude conceptions of the Christian faith. Their curas or rural clergy, their advisers, protectors, and defenders, against the injustice and persecution of their oppressors, are deeply fixed in their affections, and though strongly attached to the legendary Aztec superstitions, they yield to the Catholic creed whatever observance and reverence their uncultivated minds can be brought to comprehend.

In their present specimens of painting and carving, they still evince much of their forefathers' talent and attachment to these arts; and in their love of flowers, festivals, and music, vindicate the taste and warmth of imagination ascribed to the poetic subjects of Montezuma.

Gentle, grave, and patient, you meet them at every turn in the metropolis, plodding about the streets with their wares and merchandise, or grouped round the bazaars and pulque shops, chatting and drinking as reckless of the present as hopeless of the future. With huge panniers of vegetables, fruits, fowls, or fish, brought on their backs from ten miles' distance, and hawked from door to door till sold, they straight hie with the petty proceeds to some chapel or dramshop, to spend in masses or drink, their only resource against the pinching hunger and want of to-morrow.

Chapter XXII

*Plaza · Monté · Passion for it amongst
the Mexicans · Stoicism of the players · The
cathedral · Mexican calendar · Amusing superstition
connected with it · Virgin of Remedios · Archbishop's
and national palace · Chambers of the senate and
deputies · Museum · Cortes and Alvaro ·
Indian picture · The evangelistas ·
Monté Pio · Opera and Theatres ·
A tragedy in real life.*

The Plaza, or great square of Mexico, is fronted on the north by the cathedral and archbishop's palace, to the south of which lie the museum and market, on the east by the national palace, and on the west by the Parian or public bazaar, where every article of male or female dress in vogue amongst the people, is kept made for sale. Every interval of this square not occupied by these massive buildings is filled up with arcades, under which are small fancy stalls of flowers, books, cutlery, and bijouterie, whilst above is the Mexican palais royal of billiard and monté rooms.

This game of monté, so universally a passion with the people of the South American continent, prevails in the form of a national monomania amongst the Mexicans. Citizens of all creeds and conditions regard it as a supreme enjoyment, whose indulgence is hereditary and fixed as the laws of their being. Proscribed by law, anathematised by their religion, and carrying its desolation and ruin to the door of every family in the land, president, priest, judge, and lepero, alike pursue it with unresisting avidity, until, so far from its practice being deemed infamous, eminent and wealthy officials are known to furnish the capital of these banks, without the slightest disparagement to their standing or reputations.

In every department, state, hamlet, and city, of the country, at the scene of every festival, civil or religious, on the hacienda and ranch,

in the palace of the millionaire and the hut of the beggar, this game is introduced and played, with more or less hazard to its victims. Near a thousand of these dens are reputed to be daily open in the capital. Every cluster of hovels in the suburbs has its shrine, where tattered leperos stake at night the avails of their day's beggary, in the lowest forms of copper and silver. In the respectable cafés are those for silver alone, or gold and silver, whilst at such as are haunted by the more opulent, nothing but gold is played for, the stakers using ounces and doubloons as liberally as the cobbler risks his clacos and medios. These leading hells are said to be fitted up with taste and splendour, that vie in magnificence with any similar resorts in Europe. About them is flung an air of mystery and seclusion that accords the homage of a veil over their moral flagrancy, but those near the Plaza affect no such privacy, being owned and rented by the municipal authorities, who derive enormous revenues from their illicit use.

The early training and unintermitted habits of play, so prevalent in the very education of this people, beget an indifference to the most extravagant fluctuations of fortune that would shame the veteran habitué of Crockford's. The refined nonchalance of the caballero who has staked and lost the last farthing of his rental, or it may be his patrimonial acres themselves, is quietly reflected from the tranquil features of the peon, who with similar fortune and no less stoicism, has parted with the last rial that was to buy bread for his famished children. You look in vain from side to side of the table on which this perilous traffic of chances is conducted for the shaded brow, the writhing lip, the blanched cheek, or exultant expression of banker or bettor. There is no acting in the perfect repose of the ruined, nor a twinkle of triumph in the eyes, or tremulous vibration of the nerves, of him who pouches his sudden thousands. Where the Turkish fatalist would tear his beard, or the phlegmatic Briton seek relief in suicide, the philosophic Mexican lights his cigarito, and betakes himself unmoved to some new adventure. Calm as his glorious climate outside, whether fortune woo or disdain him, not a sigh, a smile, or exclamation, reveals his reverse or success.

Nothing can be more enchanting, as nothing is more universal with all who visit Mexico, than a view of the city from the lofty tower of the cathedral. The exterior of this edifice, though imposing, is far from realizing the purity of the Gothic style that several other churches of the republic can boast. It covers an area of five hundred feet in depth, by four hundred front, and in the magnificence of its proportions and the splendour of its decorations, extorts the admiration of all who behold it. As a single specimen of the enormous wealth of the interior, the main altar and choir is surrounded by a railing five feet high and two hundred feet in circumference, of massive thickness, and composed of solid gold and silver, and surmounted at short distances with silver statues of saints and apostles, for holding tapers during the service. The altar itself is of pure silver, wrought and chased in the most beautiful style, and covered with a profusion of weighty vessels of gold and silver of countless value. Above, in a miniature temple, is the genuine figure of the Virgin of Remedios, wearing a dress of diamonds and precious stones, whose lowest value is estimated at three millions of dollars.

Leaning against a buttress of one of the towers outside, is a great circular mass of basalt, called the El Relox de Montezuma, or watch of Montezuma. This is the famous calendar of which so many learned descriptions and translations have been furnished to the world by the antiquarians who have seen it. It was disinterred in the Plaza, and is covered with astronomical symbols and hieroglyphics, illustrating the progress of the aborigines in the science of astronomy. Both the sculpture and accuracy of its computations are thought greatly to excel those of any similar monuments of art perfected by the Greeks or Romans. This calendar but represents half the year, the remaining segment being contained on a similar stone, which is reported to lie at the depth of about twelve feet from the surface, beneath a pedestal supporting a cross, near the cathedral. Superstition has kept it there, and superstition will hold it locked in its sepulchre, until the advance of an enlightened sentiment emancipates the public mind from its unworthy thraldom. In connexion with these and other carved stones found in various parts of this valley, Baron Humboldt relates an amusing superstition, growing out of their imperfect calculations, that prevailed amongst the aborigines.

At the termination of their cycle of fifty-two years, they believed the sun would be extinguished, and in his stead their evil gods would descend and destroy the earth. Unlike the Latter Day Saints of modern times, they looked for an indiscriminate destruction, maugre all Apocalyptic exceptions of sanctity, election, ascension robes, or other accessories of escape.

On the arrival of the portentous day that concluded their great cycle, the sacred fires of their temples were extinguished, their property destroyed, their garments rent in twain, and the whole land filled to its uttermost extremities with howls and execrations of despair. A solemn compunction and dread sprung up in the minds of the men from their women, believing that the latter were to be transformed into ferocious beasts that would unite with the coming demons, and revenge themselves on their faithless husbands and lovers, for their injustice and neglect. Such as were pregnant were objects of peculiar horror, and these they covered with disguises and locked up, to prevent their recognition and alliance with their foes. When the night of the last day arrived, the priests clothed themselves in the dress of their idols, and followed by the frantic populace, went out in procession to a mountain six miles from Mexico. This procession was termed the New Fire, and having ascended to the summit of the mountain, they watched until the Pleiades ascended to the zenith, and then commenced a sacrifice of human victims. A man was laid upon his back on the altar of sacrifice, and his heart covered with a wooden shield, which the priest ignited by friction. As soon as the victim was killed, a machine to kindle fire was put in motion over the shield on his breast. When a blaze was thus created, it was communicated to a pile of combustibles previously prepared, whose illumination was a signal to those in the city and on the look-out, that the gods had reprieved the world and its inhabitants for another cycle. Couriers stationed near each other, communicated this joyful intelligence to the despairing populace of every village in the empire, and the sun that rose on the morrow in confirmation of their pardon, was hailed and celebrated by acclamations and feasts.

The archbishop's and president's palaces are large but unadorned buildings, with less architectural pretension than taste and sumptuousness in their interior furnish. Behind the national palace stands the Capitol, or halls of the Senate and Chamber of Deputies, commodious and handsome apartments; and in their immediate vicinity the mint, where most of the coinage of the republic is executed.

A gloomy and monastic pile close by is pointed out as the prison of the Inquisition, within whose dark and vaulted recesses the murders and tortures of that bloodstained and pitiless tribunal were of old inflicted.

The National Museum, dedicated to the preservation of the parsimonious fragments of Mexican art and history which have been

recovered from the wreck of the past, is a splendid suite of apartments, but exhibiting the most culpable neglect in the custodian
to whom they are committed. Portraits of the viceroys and old Spanish monarchs, fragments of thrones and armour, are jumbled without order or arrangement, amongst Mexican idols, mummies,
masks, and monsters. Vases and altars, cups and monkish manu-
scripts, antique Spanish coins, and Indian drums and whistles, lie
about in grotesque disorder, challenging as much labour in their inspection, as was devoted to their exhumation and collection. By far
the most interesting relic to all but the archæological enthusiast,
are the veritable suits of mail of Cortes and Alvaro. They are both
plain and simple steel harness, and that of the former adapted to the
frame of a man of medium height and ordinary proportions. A genuine likeness of Cortes in his viceroyal dress, is likewise amongst the
portraits, portraying the characteristic dignity and firmness of the
martial bigot, who swam through such incarnadine seas of human
butchery, to win this glorious empire to the cross and crown of
Spain. Opposite his picture hangs a large gold frame, covered with
glass, containing the banner under which he had fought his bloody
conflicts, and under whose holy sign all his enormities were perpetrated. It represents the celestial Virgin on a field of crimson silk,
surrounded with stars, and blazoned with the inscription of Con-
stantine,

In hoc signo vinces.

Near it, and arranged as though to mock the affected sanctity of
the hero and his motto, is an Indian painting, illustrating one out of
the many cruelties employed to strike terror into the hearts of the
simple people whom he had subjugated. In one corner it represents
the conqueror, accompanied by Donna Marina, his Mexican mis-
tress. The latter holds a rosary suspended from her uplifted hand,
raised in an attitude of supplication, whilst her lover seems in the
act of issuing a command, whose execution is explained by the remaining figures of the group. These exhibit a Spanish soldier holding by a long chain attached to a ferocious bloodhound, whose fangs
are fixed in the throat of an Indian. The colours faithfully delineate
the horror and suffering of the victim, who, with hair erect, and
mouth and eyes distended, seems the very embodiment of mortal
anguish. The streaming blood, and gashes on various portions of the
body, make out the rude but eloquent narrative of the savage record.

Amongst the multitudes that throng the vicinity of the Parian, and gossip and traffic round its numerous shops, the evangelistas or professional letter-writers, attract no inconsiderable attention from the curious stranger. Seated on low portable stools on the edge of the pavement, a board across their knees for a writing-desk, on which is ink and various piles of coloured paper, these grave, learned, and confidential scribes are to be found, ever at their post, ready to indite missives of business or sentiment, as the humour of the applicants require. Poetry or prose, a billet-doux or a sonnet, an elegy or epitaph, are equally within their line, and all or any executed with an expedition commensurate with the necessity of the case. Their clerkly apparel of sable frocks and slouched hats, their intellectual, sympathizing, sentimental expression of countenance, their pantomimic tact, ready apprehension, and quiet tones, all conspire to win their way at once to the confidence of such as feel dependent on their craft. A fund of entertainment is open to the idle observer, who cares to note the language of eyes and gesticulation that passes between one of these amanuenses and a customer. Cheaply and efficiently do they supply the remissness of the schoolmaster, to many an unfortunate wight and damsel, delineating the most majestic or tender emotions of the soul, at prices so reduced as to render such records accessible to all who crave them. Should the matter to be communicated be one of distress, the evangelista can scarce proceed for his sympathetic sensibility; should it prove a blushing narrative of passion, the insinuating delicacy of his glances reassures and sustains the timid narrator; and if rage or disdain be its theme, it is easy to interpret from his flashing eye and rapid chirography, how fully embarked he feels in the services of his employer. Treasurers of more numerous and important secrets than the confessor, they come to be held in great regard, and rarely are they passed without the most affectionate recognition by such as have been the recipients of their aid.

The palace of Cortes, said to be erected on the ruins of that of Montezuma, is now appropriated to the use of the Monte Pio, or national pawnbroker institution. This establishment, richly endowed and managed by a board of directors, is reputed to be administered with great fidelity and impartiality, dispensing its beneficent relief to the needy thousands whose daily exigencies drive them to its counter. Every species of valuable and property that is not perishable in its nature, is appraised at a fair valuation when presented here, and the amount (exclusive of interest) paid the owner and the property retained in pledge. Within six months this pawn can be redeemed by the pawner's reimbursing the amount, but if not redeemed within that period, it is auctioned off to the highest bidder, and the excess if any, restored to the owner. More than half a million of dollars is annually loaned in this form to some forty thousand persons; the beggar and noble, the lady and her maid, as often registered amongst its beneficiaries.

Notwithstanding the ardent musical taste that pervades all classes of the population, the opera cannot be brought to succeed in Mexico, despite the enterprise which has been more than once displayed in its behalf. But such is their love for their theatres that they literally live in them. These are three in number: the Principal, the Nuevo Mexico, and the Puente Quebrada. The former is the resort of the aristocracy, and the two latter under the more particular patronage of the toiling million. The taste of the audiences is inexorably fixed upon the broadest comedy, or that melodramatic sentimentality, revealed through plots of love and murder, roguery and piracy. Their native dramatic muse has not risen as yet to any reputable inspiration, so that their national taste is still left dependent upon the threadbare repetition or irregular offspring of the Spanish school. The dress, scenery, music, and accommodations of the houses, are all upon the most respectable footing, and the crowded attendance such as must speedily enrich the management.

A tragedy of real life was enacted some three years since in the dressing-room of the Nuevo Mexico, that though stifled in some of its atrocious details by those interested in its suppression, inspired a pity and indignation at the time, unequalled by any of the mimic horrors accustomed to be rehearsed within its walls. A native girl of Zacatecas, of rarest talent and loveliness, the natural daughter of a distinguished officer of the revolution, had displayed such decided and extraordinary gifts for the profession, as induced her friends to gratify her in the adoption of it. Her enthusiasm and taste, united with her graces of person and manner, not only bewitched all the caballeros of the dress circle, but unfortunately drew on her the admiration of a married comedian of Castile, who with his young and doting wife was at the time connected with the dramatis personæ of the establishment. This attachment, wholly confined to the enamoured comico, became soon revealed to the jealous vigilance of his wife, who, fired with revenge towards its innocent object, approached her in the dressing-room during an interlude in the play, and taxing the trembling debutante with her despair, cast a vial of vitriol over her face and bosom.

The young artiste survived her disfigurement but a few weeks; and her penitent destroyer expiated her unhappy deed by taking poison in the Accordada a few days after her arrest.

Chapter XXIII

*National religion · Murder of Hayden · Passage
of the Host · Estates of the Church before and since
the Revolution · Number of the clergy and conventual
establishments · Character of the Mexican clergy ·
Festival of the Virgin of Guadaloupe · Festival
of the Virgin of Remedios.*

The Catholic religion is the established religion of Mexico, and no other form of worship is tolerated or practised. Not a chapel dedicated to the service of another faith is open within the boundaries of the republic; and so prejudiced and bigoted is the state of public sentiment, that the diplomatic corps from Protestant countries *dare not* celebrate the rites of their creed out of the recesses of their own dwellings.

During the fiercest days of the revolution, when a wholesale hatred of Old Spain, and her tyrannical abuses, reigned supreme in the popular heart—when a bias towards royalty brought many a monk to a bloody end, this intolerant jealousy of Protestantism displayed itself in the following lawless proceeding.

An American Protestant, Mr. Hayden, a shoemaker by trade, had settled in the city to prosecute his calling. A rigid observer of the Catholic ceremonies and institutions in his outward deportment, he yet clung to the tenets of the reformed faith in which he had been reared, decorously yet firmly professing them within the sanctuary of his humble home. The host passing his shop one day, to the bedside of some dying Catholic, he came forward to his doorway and knelt, in conformity with the requirements of the country. Whilst thus prostrated, a person accompanying the procession, and armed with a sword, came forward and demanded of him why he had not advanced into the street and paid his homage there. Hayden, apprehending an assault upon his person, rose to retreat within his house, when he was stabbed through the back, and instantly killed. The murderer fled from an American present, who sought to apprehend him, and the crowd closing around defended him from arrest.

Permission was next refused by the authorities to the application of our consul to bury him, and granted only on condition of his being interred at Chapultepec, near two leagues distant from the city. No coachman would take the heretical corpse in his carriage, and the consul was obliged to receive it in his own. A mob gathered round the dwelling of the deceased in formidable numbers, and pursued the funeral train along the streets, pelting it with missiles, until the consul procured a military guard for its escort to the grave. At the grave the consul was stoned whilst reading the service, notwith-standing the presence of the soldiers, and though a hired watch was set over the sepulchre, it was the same night broken open, and the corpse stripped of its shroud and clothes, and flung out upon the ground. The resident foreigners offered a reward of *two thousand dollars* for the murderer and violators of the tomb, but they were never informed against or punished.

You are in the most crowded and bustling street of the city, thronged with grandees, soldiers, merchants, chapmen, porters, and leperos, and the Babel hum of a thousand voices comes like a roll of drums upon your ear. A coach, drawn by four white or spotted mules, containing a priest in his sacerdotal robes, and escorted on either side by bands of boys in white tunics, chaunting a hymn,

turns a corner of the square and approaches; it is the host, on its way to the chamber of death. In a moment every head is uncovered, and the whole crowd on their knees, where they stand, in murmuring prayer. The silence of the grave has fallen upon the street, save the dirge-like voices of the youthful choir. A neighbouring angle shuts the holy mystery from view, and in a trice the silent and motionless crowd are on their feet, as intent on this world and its concerns as before.

From the date of the conquest to that of the revolution, the policy of the Spanish government aimed to extend the power and temporalities of the Mexican church to their highest point of advancement. In no country under the sun, where St. Peter laid claim to patrimony, did his priesthood and property augment with such rapidity, and increase, as in Mexico. The estates of the church, consisting of lands and houses, in town and country, churches, convents, monasteries, plate, furniture, jewels, and active funds, which are now computed at *one hundred millions of dollars*, had then attained, under royal influence, to a third more in the value of the realty, beside, one hundred and fifteen millions of dollars of capital, accumulated by contributions and impost of tithes, levied upon the *universal* property of the country. Thirteen thousand ecclesiastics of various orders swarmed over the land, united and indivisible in the promotion of the wealth and authority of their system. Insatiable in avarice, and inflexible in the prosecution of their aggrandizements, they annually increased their gains from dying penitents, pious bequests, and votive offerings. Whilst bigoted viceroys shared the administration of their temporal power with haughty and ambitious prelates in the capital, combining their bayonets with the omnipotent terrors of the holy office, in shrouding their joint despotism from scrutiny, the village *curés*, acting under the influence of one scheming and powerful head, penetrated every Indian hut and hamlet, propagating a blind submission and observance to every behest of their powerful chapter.

The revolution came, and by the proscriptions and exactions of rival and contending factions, materially reduced the numbers and revenues of the fraternity. The tithe system was abolished, enormous loans, forced from their coffers for the maintenance of the war, and the rights of primogeniture being destroyed, divorced the alliance of clergy and nobles, by shutting the church-preferments from the younger sons of the latter, which had previously bound them in a defensive confederation. But though greatly diminished in power and splendour, and tending to a more radical reform, if not an entire prostration, the establishment is yet formidable not only for its great wealth, but for that affection and influence its past character and benevolences have won for it in the hearts of the unenlightened mass.

Seven thousand clergy, monks, and nuns, represent the spiritual wants of the country, and control the remaining wealth of the church, of $100,000,000. These may be divided into two thousand nuns, one thousand five hundred monks, and three thousand six hundred secular clergy, whose conventual retreats consist of fifty-eight nunneries, and one hundred and fifty monasteries. The daring hand of sacrilege having already been laid so heavily upon their toil-some savings, has not only subjected them to the dread of farther confiscation, but stimulates the needy and greedy government to frequently contemplate their entire appropriation. The alarming co-incidence is often referred to of the national debt and the church property being nearly equal in amount, and suggestions are publicly made, that as these estates were collected for the purposes of char-ity, no better object can be found than the pauper republic, on which to lavish them. The vows of chastity and poverty assumed by the clergy, make such enormous revenues hostile to the pure practice of religion, and patriotism being a paramount duty in the inculcations of Christianity, points to an empty exchequer as the most appropri-ate channel in which to divert them.

If the spirit of the Christian creed could be degraded or polluted by the conduct of its professors, the licentiousness of many of the holy fathers of the Mexican capital would go far to effect such a result. To say nothing of the many profligate indulgences attributed to them, their unabashed appearance at the gaming-tables and billiard-rooms, the bull-fights and cafés, and other resorts of vice and infamy, open-ly and in full dress, participating in their abandoned amusements, and boldly sanctioning their corruptions, has done much to divest them of that respect and reverence due the sacred ministry they so vilely scandalize. There is great worth and merit (as before intimat-ed) in the rural clergy, most of whom not only practise a pious self-denial, and honest devotion to the service of God, but are active in the exercise of all generous humanities to the poor, the afflicted, and the oppressed.

These are too few and dispersed, however, to be said to redeem the tarnished fame of the Mexican church, as none but the more devoted and pious will encounter the sacrifices incident to these humble walks. By far the larger portion are to be found swarmed in the cities, where affluence, ease, and unrestrained luxury, present attractive snares to willing appetite.

A pontifical bull of recent date has greatly limited the number of their holidays, but the gay population are still permitted more than appertain to other Catholic countries. Amongst these the festivals of the Virgin of Guadaloupe, and the Virgin of Remedios, are by far the most popular and attractive.

That of the former occurs on the 12th of December, at her magnificent shrine some three miles north of the city. Here thousands upon thousands of every rank and condition, from the president and archbishop down to the Indian and lepero, annually assemble to celebrate the rites of this patron saint of Mexico. The consecration of the day above mentioned to these solemnities, is thus explained in a legend, gravely rehearsed by the archbishop himself, and as gravely received by his pious audience upon each recurring anniversary.

Some few years after the conquest, as a converted Indian watched his browsing flock, at the base of the sterile mountain of Tepeyac, the most Holy Virgin suddenly stood before him in *propria persona*. She instructed him to go to the Bishop of Mexico, and in her name command him to come and worship her on the site of the present church. This heavenly visitation occurred at midday on the 9th of December. The wondering shepherd acquitted him forthwith of his commission, and on the following day the Virgin was punctual to the hour to hear the result. The ambassador having informed her of his failure to obtain an audience with the bishop, was again commanded on a similar errand, with the explanatory injunction, that it was Mary, the Mother of God, who sent him. The Indian executed his errand with somewhat better success, but returned with the report that the bishop refused to believe his tale, unless he brought some credential to satisfy him of the authority of his commission. On the 12th of December, for the third time, she appeared to her messenger, and ordered him to ascend the barren mountain, and bring her some roses he would find in bloom at a designated spot. What was the astonishment of the incredulous but obedient shepherd to find the roses as described, where vegetation had never before appeared. Having brought them to the Virgin, she threw them into the Indian's apron, telling him to show them to the bishop, as the credentials of his embassy. When arrived in the presence of the monk he unfolded his apron, and there appeared stamped on the garment an exquisitely wrought picture of the Blessed Virgin herself. Each petal of the flowers bore a similar image to that on the apron, which has been preserved ever since without the slightest decay of tint or material, and is now adorned with costly gems, and hung up in the altar of the church in a gold frame with a crystal face. The Virgin appeared a fourth time to her ambassador, and after rewarding him with various benedictions, admonished that the name to be given to the saint of the apron was the Virgin of Guadaloupe.

A splendid church was immediately founded on the spot pointed out in the annunciation, and the shrine is now deemed one of the richest in the world.

Rude copies of the portrait are to be found in every hovel in Mexico, and the original acknowledged as the presiding divinity of the republic.

On the side of the mountain opposite the chapel of Guadaloupe, towers a lofty brick wall, about thirty feet wide and seventy high. Its erection is thus explained: a wealthy Mexican merchant and family returning from abroad by sea, was overtaken by a violent storm that for several days threatened to overwhelm the ship and crew. Appalled by the imminent peril that threatened him, the merchant betook him to the customary invocation of the saints, and in the extremity of his love of life vowed to rear another temple to his patroness of Guadaloupe, if she would have pity on their jeopardy. The impending destruction was averted, the wind abated, and the ship and its crew arrived safely at its destined port. In place of redeeming his vow with pious fidelity, the faithless votary compromised his plighted munificence, by putting up this semblance of a sail, a memento of his rescue and perfidy.

The festival of the Virgin of Remedios, though originally sprung from Spanish superstition, has long been consigned to the exclusive celebration of the Indians. It was instituted in commemoration of the following plausible event. When the Spaniards were expelled from Mexico on the famous *noche triste* (or sad night), they retreated some distance to the mountains and encamped. The morning after this night of panic and disaster, a doll was found on an aloe, placed there by some officer familiar with the ready superstition of the Spanish soldiery. It was straightway proclaimed a miraculous image of the Holy Virgin, dropped from heaven in token of its future favour to the arms of the cross. When the conquest was accomplished, a church was founded on the spot where the toy was found, and the doll taken to sanctuary under the title of the Virgin of Remedios.

Under her especial patronage are all the ills of life. The sick, the sorrowful, and unlucky, invoke her remedial aid in every visitation that befalls them. The farmers seek her interposition against protracted drought or wet; and districts infected with pestilence or epidemics, have been known to hire the presence of her sanctified image at the rate of thousands per day.

The church in which the festival in honour of this saint is celebrated stands on the unsheltered side of the mountain, and though once a tasteful edifice, is now more than half in ruins. The genuine image of the Virgin, the object of these idolatrous rites, has long since been removed to the cathedral in Mexico; where the tempting gems on her ladyship's robe are deemed more secure than in the mountains.

A counterfeit doll is substituted in her place, and the cheat (if known) quietly acquiesced in and as cordially adorned by the simple-minded Indians.

Chapter XXIV

*Mexican vagrancy · Fraternity of thieves
and robbers · Affair at the Adouana · Colonel
Janes and Santa Anna · The Ladrones and their
mode of operation · Madame Castellan and the
American Minister · Mexican morgue · The
Accordada · The Garotte · Female
convicts.*

With a climate whose voluptuous mildness irresistibly inclines to sloth, and a soil whose spontaneous productions would suffice of themselves to sustain a frugal people, it is not astonishing that vagrancy in all its forms, from genteel loaferism to the lowest vagabondism, should so widely diffuse itself amongst the Mexicans. Ardent and impulsive in temperament, passionately devoted to enjoyment and susceptible to its every lure, they plunge with reckless extravagance into costly excesses, heedless of all prudential maxims where their humours are enlisted. In the capital you meet porters, charcoal venders, and aguadors, plodding from door to door the length of the entire city, under burdens that would start the tears from a mule; and at night you will not fail to encounter them lavishing their earnings at any public resort you may visit. The ruined cavalier or bankrupt tradesmen, have none of that recuperative energy that reconstructs a fortune squandered by waste or lost by mischance. The ill-luck that overtakes them once, robs them at the same time of capital and calling. No outward manifestations of despair are visible, but all further application to regular and legitimate business is over, and if other less desperate resources fail them, the highway or monté table must supply their necessities and cater to their pleasures.

Among the numerous wretches who, as professional beggars, swarm the streets of this city, or in the filthy guise of blackened leperos, haunt the pavement by day, and prowl for plunder at night, are outcasts and cut-throats, whom previous convictions have deadened to all sense of shame, and habitual vice and indolence trained to every deed of violence. In the portals of the churches, beneath the walls of the convents, in the markets, or their lairs in the suburbs, they crouch to watch for their unsuspecting prey, and wo to that unarmed pedestrian, who, in reply to their *Por el amor de Dios*, reveals a purse to tempt their ferocious cupidity.

Banded in fraternities, that reach from the pulque shops to the palace, their organization has been known to reveal itself through every grade of rank, from the roofless footpad to those nearest in authority to the president. An instance of audacity is authentically related to have occurred some years ago, which not unaptly illustrates the lawless spirit of these plunderers. The mules of a conducta were ranged in two files in the square of Adouana (or custom-house), and, surrounded by a strong squadron of cavalry, waited to be loaded with the bags of specie, containing fifteen hundred dollars each, and piled up in the square to be sent off. A large crowd was as usual assembled to look on, when a gang of mounted thieves charged through the streets leading to the square, and riding down idlers and troops, seized each a bag of the treasure, and bore it off in triumph.

The energy of the present government has done much to reduce the frequency and insolence of these outrages about the capital, yet they continue to prevail in all their wonted atrocity elsewhere through the republic. Not a league of their only national highway from the city to Vera Cruz, but is the scene of some robbery within the year, the public coach being repeatedly pillaged within hail of the cities that lie on the route.

The following notorious instance of a participation in these enormities by persons of rank, is familiar to all persons of inquiry who have recently been in Mexico.

The Swiss consul, (M. Mairet,) a merchant and man of fortune, lived in the western suburbs of the city, and was suspected to have a considerable sum of money about his house. His dwelling was more than ordinarily secure, being built in the strongest manner, with grated windows, and several ferocious dogs kept chained in the court and on the terrace.

A man in the habit of a priest, accompanied by two others, appeared at his gate one day, and announced to the servant, who answered their summons, that they desired to purchase some merchandise of the consul, in which he was known to deal. Upon being admitted, two of them seized the servant, bound him to a pillar, and gagged him, whilst the third relocked the gate. All three then passed into the house, where they found Mairet alone, and, after stabbing and gashing him repeatedly, finally compelled him to disclose the place where his treasure was secreted. This, to the amount of ten thousand dollars, with various articles of valuable plate, they brought off; the consul only surviving his wounds long enough to relate the particulars of the affair, with such descriptions of the assassins, as it was thought would lead to their apprehension. A noisy search and pursuit was kept up by the police, until a miserable creature was arrested, tried, and garroted, upon the ground of some declarations said to have fallen from him whilst grossly intoxicated. No money or article of the plunder being found in his possession, nor any corroborative circumstance accompanying his insane confession, the foreigners denounced the execution as a cowardly subterfuge of the government to atone for its corruption or remissness by a *double* murder.

Some time elapsed, when two daring robberies were again perpetrated in rapid succession upon wealthy monasteries of the city. These were entered and pillaged of more than thirty thousand dollars, and the church being roused and combined in the pursuit with the civil authorities, finally traced them home to the door of Colonel Janes, an officer of standing, and acting aide-de-camp of General Santa Anna. This worthy colonel, having access to the passport office, was more than suspected of having planned several previous robberies of the public coach, availing himself of the information thus acquired to direct his accomplices where the booty was such as to indemnify an attack.

The trial of himself and associates for the pillage of the monasteries lasted nearly three years, every effort being made during this time, by Santa Anna and other officials, to screen him from conviction. Their attempts, however, proving abortive, and sentence of death being finally awarded against him, it fell to the lot of the dictator, who had, in the meanwhile, risen to the presidency, to ratify the verdict, and order his execution. This he declined to do, upon one pretext and another, granting the condemned respite after respite, until popular indignation became exasperated to the highest pitch. Dreading the fury his equivocal course had excited in the

public mind, and alarmed by threats of a revolutionary character, Santa Anna retired from the city, and left the task of consummating the vengeance of the law to General Bravo.

Janes was finally executed, and, before suffering, confessed his numerous crimes. Amongst these was the murder of Mairet, in which, as in all, he plead the connivance of Santa Anna, and other accomplices. He died, invoking the most direful curses upon their heads, for abandoning him and concurring in his death. His assertions were ridiculed as the malicious coinage of a desperate felon, by those whose interest it was to discredit them, but public sentiment received them with credit at the time, and the same impression continues with thousands yet.

The Ladrones who infest the highway to Vera Cruz, are more humanized than their associates on other roads, rarely murdering unless resistance is made, and never assailing where they are not certain of a respectable booty. The arrieros, who transport upon the backs of their mules all the interior commerce of the country, are seldom molested, travelling through all dangerous districts in caravans of from fifty to a hundred, and besides being on friendly footing with their unscrupulous countrymen, are known to be determined and intrepid fellows. Another reason for their impunity, is the disdain of the banditti for all cumbrous plunder, preferring the more valuable and portable pillage to be found on the persons of travellers.

Having agents in all the cities and towns on the road, the most exact information is given them of the number, character, baggage, and supposed wealth of the passengers, how armed, and the probable nature of the defence that will be offered to their exactions. With this knowledge, they are enabled to despatch their operation with considerable precision and expedition.

By the side of some wooded barranca, the ambushed gang await the arrival of the coach, and unless escorted by a faithful guard, bring it to a halt by firing a shot over the head of the driver.

The Jehu, if a Mexican, may be always regarded as on the most amiable terms with the freebooters, and assents to the startling *Hal-to! quien va allia?* that follows the discharge of the carbine, by promptly reining up, and civilly responding *Amigos! señors, como esta vend?* delivered in a tone as cordial as though he was discoursing his next landlord. In a moment the coach is surrounded, and whilst the leader and his lieutenant open the door and invite the travellers to descend, a dozen or twenty musket muzzles ogle them through every aperture of the vehicle. The male cargo are one by one relieved at the foot of the steps, of cloaks, serapes, watches, rings, purses, and pocket-books, by the officers. They are then handed over to the men, who conduct them as fast as received some few paces off, and making them lie down on their faces, continue the examination by drawing their boots and manipulating their legs, arms, and bodies, as though they were feeling for the seat of some acute pain. When their examination is through with, and as they lie tranquilly in line at full length on the earth, they strongly resemble so many Mecca pilgrims prostrated in the desert before the approach of an advancing sirocco.

It is not to be presumed that the gallantry of these contrabandistas (their avarice consenting) allows a less affectionate examination of the ladies, if there be any, than is paid to their lords. Their unknightly reversal of the usual chronology of good breeding in devoting their first attentions to these heroes, by no means involves a less strict or punctilious compliment to the fair. A refinement of delicacy alone procures for the latter an impartial and private inquest, unembarrassed and influenced by the presence of their protectors. *Buenos noche, señoras, duermen vendes! es tiempo de despertar*, may be heard from the courteous montanes, as they enter the coach and rouse the trembling covey of spinsters inside. *Su bolsa, si le gusta vend*, and so on, including *los anillos, zarcillos, brazaletes, sortijas, mantillas*, and even *el abanico*, if they have one. Next comes a search of the *zagalejo, el bonete, la cotilla, los guantes, zapatos, y midias*, amidst struggles, entreaties, tears, and blushes, on one side, and oaths and protestations on the other.

The picaroon captain having completed his work of spoliation, departs with the most courteous expressions of regret, saluting the coach and his prostrate victims, with *Adios! señors, y señoritas! Voya con dios, hasta que encontremos otra vez*, facetiously begging to be remembered to the nearest authorities, civil and military.

If the travellers be foreigners and well armed, it is not often they are interrupted, as the report of fire-arms may bring up some of the cavalry patrol, who scour the country for the suppression of these bravos.

A few years since, the diligence, containing the celebrities of the operatic corps, on their way to Mexico, was stopped, and the passengers stript of all their money and luggage. The Prima Donna (Madame Castellan) was relieved of near ten thousand dollars, in cash and jewels, and constrained by the musical brigands to warble them some of her sweetest cadenzas before parting.

The past summer a similar misfortune befell the new American minister on his way to the capital, being compelled to a horizontal prostration of his concentrated sanctity and sovereignty, whilst his ambassadorial pouches were rifled of their last dime.

Notwithstanding the enormous amount of roguery and robbery that goes unwhipt of justice in Mexico, scarce a prison inside it but is literally stocked with malefactors. The Accordada or public prison of the capital stands in the western part of the city, and never contains within its capacious dimensions less than from five to ten thousand criminals. A basement room in one of its wings, with a grated window opening on the street, is used as a morgue or dead room, where the bodies of persons slain in the city and suburbs during the night are collected, and brought next morning for recognition and interment by their friends. The statement may seem incredible to those unacquainted with the prevalence of murder and assassination here, but not less than six hundred bodies are thus annually exposed, since the commencement of the revolution. Every morning an anxious and melancholy crowd may be seen assembled around this gloomy window, inspecting the interior or waiting the further report of the police, to learn tidings of some friend, relative, or domestic, who is missing.

Entering through the numerous guards and sentinels on duty before the portals of this prison, you ascend a stair to the second story, where in a lofty apartment are the turnkeys and various officers who have charge of the establishment. The clank of chains, and the frightful din of the loathsome Babel, almost deafens the visiter on reaching this landing. Passing from here through a half-dozen ponderous, iron-barred doors, you come to an elevated corridor, circuiting an immense quadrangular court-yard, crammed with human beings of all ages and appearances, from the boyish stripling to the palsied dotard. In the centre is a filthy fountain, swarming with naked felons in their bath, whilst a hundred separate crowds of burglars, murderers, ravishers, poisoners, forgers, footpads, and adulterers, are gathered in different occupations of relaxation or labour. Here a group is formed round the narrator of some bloody feat of violence, and there another shouting their bravos round a witty storyteller. Here a cluster of squalid wretches are watching the progress of a game of monté, played with cards nearly illegible from grease, and using frijoles or bread balls for counters, and there another weaving coarse rebosos in hand-looms. So unleavened, redemptionless, hardened, and repulsive a hive of villains, are no where else to be met with on earth.

In one corner of the square is the chapel, where those under sentence of death are condemned to penance and solitude, during the last three days of life. Whilst undergoing this solemn punishment, (almost as dreadful as the death that awaits them,) their fellow-convicts gather round the door of the chapel at twilight of each day, and chaunt a *miserere* for the departing soul of their comrade.

All punishments of death awarded by the law are inflicted by the garotte. The culprit being seated in a chair against an upright post, an iron collar, attached to the latter, is fastened round his neck, which may be contracted by means of a screw. The prisoner receives the last shrift from the attending priest after he is bound in the chair, and a necessary compression of the collar is obtained. At the conclusion of the prayer by the padre, the executioner gives the fatal turn to the screw, and a spike, inside the collar, penetrating the spinal marrow at the same time, extinguishes life immediately. No mode of execution can be more humane and less revolting than the garotte. The ghastly apparatus of the gibbet, or the guillotine, find no reflex in the simple and unappalling stake and chair. The prisoner walks to the terminus of his life's journey unbound and accompanied by his friends and relatives, if they desire it. Seated in the chair, with a cowl over his neck and head, he looks at the worst, as only about to undergo an operation of dentistry or ophthalmia. When the eyes of the surrounding crowd, bent under their devotions, are lifted up to look upon the dying struggle, it is over, and not a heave of the trunk, a groan, or the quiver of a limb, betrays that the dissolution of soul and body has transpired.

The prison for the women adjoins, but is separate from that of the males. Its arrangement is the same, but a more enlightened and humane discipline pervades it. *Nine hundred* of these wretched outcasts were said to be confined, on charges as heinous and more varied than the men, and *three* were at the time under condemnation for murder and poisoning!

Chapter XXV

The Alameda · Santa Anna · The
Passeo Nuevo · Bull-fights · Departure
from Mexico · The corpse and cross · Town of
Perote · Visit to the Castle · Sufferings of the prisoners ·
Their memorial to Mr. Bankhead · Their
liberation · Mr. Navarro.

If the stranger would see the rank, beauty, wealth, and style of the capital to advantage, he must stroll west to the Alameda, about four o'clock in the afternoon. Passing through a street almost entirely filled by French jewellers, French fancy shops, *modistes* and *artistes*, he comes upon a beautiful grove of twelve or fifteen acres, planted with the noblest trees of the southern forests, and filled with the rarest shrubbery and flowers. A stone wall encircles this delicious retreat, which is entered through gates, that are opened and closed morning and evening by janitors appointed to the care of them. Gravelled walks and winding paths intersect it in every direction, and marble fountains, in secluded nooks, fling up their silvery *jets d'eau*, that mingle their falling murmurs with the melody of numerous birds inhabiting the wood. A statue of Liberty, surrounded by spouting lions, surmounts the central fountain, whilst tasteful stone seats every where invite the visiter to repose.

Within its quiet and druidical recesses, you encounter the sable mourner and sentimental *amante*, drawn hither to luxuriate in melting revery, over buried and newborn affection; or, the student and merchant, to refresh their energies by an hour's walk amongst its genial shades.

A broad carriage-road runs round the interior wall, and not a belle of Mexico but is here every evening, chatting and flirting from her dashing equipage, with the numerous cavaliers who throng it, on superb and splendidly equipped-horses. Slowly the beauty and chivalry of the city circuit the dense and refreshing shade, until the clanking sabres and tramping hoofs of an approaching guard, admonish them to draw up on the side of the way. The caballeros have reined back in lines, the coaches are hugging the walls, and grot and fountain have poured out their pensive *habitués* to the edge of the wood, when in dash fifty hussars, five abreast, followed by a coach, flashing with gold and crimson, and drawn by four mettlesome bloods, driven by a coachman in gorgeous livery. An equal number of hussars, in similar order, follow in the rear of the coach, whilst on each side caracole three aide-de-camps, caparisoned, man and horse, in the most splendid style. The coach and its escort move slowly around the enclosure, and as it passes every hat is off, and fans and fair heads are moved in graceful salutation of its solitary occupant. The object of this homage is a military dignitary, dressed in a uniform of blue and gold, and blazing with medals and diamond decorations suspended from his neck. His arms are folded on his bosom, *à la Napoleon*, and he nods his unplumed *chapeau de oras* in haughty acknowledgment of the civilities received. It is Don Antonio Lopez de Santa Anna, President of the Republic.

At the western gate of the Alameda the cavalcade turns out, and enters the Passeo Nuevo, another lung of the metropolis, bordered for a mile with shaded paths, and adorned with fountains, sculpture, and statuary. The fashionables follow in lengthened procession, and the Alameda is deserted and silent, but for its doves and fountains.

The moonlight of Mexico is so pure and radiantly bright, the atmosphere so rarefied, and the blue sky above so intensely blue, that no medium seems to interpose between the dazzling constellations on high, and the earth they shine upon. Bathed in such pellucid light, you think you can see the spiral thread of smoke that issues from Popocatepetl, thirty-three miles off, and mark the very spot where it melts against the background of the sky. On nights like these, the temples and towers of the city stand out defined in every petty outline, and you would bet on counting each lash in the lids of those dreamy eyes, that look down on you from the bloom-clad azoteas. The prowler and the stabber are in bed, for their lurks are lit up as with noonday's glare; the old monasteries fling but half a shadow from their walls; and so still and deathlike is the reign of silence, that you list to hear the stroke of the scourge as it comes from the midnight penitentia of the monk.

Bull-fights, the boasted recreation of their fathers, have been long on the decline amongst the Mexicans, the matador and picador,

though of the most genuine Andalusian stamp and training, finding dull employment for their brutal skill, except amongst the distant cities and villages. The Plaza de Toros, an immense circus erected when this sport was in its palmy popularity, is now seldom opened, few beside leperos and idlers attending an exhibition when it comes off. The lords of lowing herds are thus left by this revolution of public taste to the more tender mercies of the lasso.

In the square of the university is a beautiful equestrian bronze statue of Charles IV., cast by a native artist. The costume of the monarch is Roman, the laurel wreath, imperial robe, tunic, buskins, and antique sword and truncheon, being executed with faultless precision. The horse is of colossal size, and the proportions admirable. It is considered by critics a master-piece of art, and is thought to contrast most favourably with the best specimen of its kind extant, from the chisels of the old masters.

The clanking bells were calling the devout of the city to early mass, on the last morning of June, as, comfortably accoutred and provided against all mishaps on the road, I passed out through the Puerto de San Lazaro, on my way to Vera Cruz. At the door of a miserable hovel in the suburb near this portal, stood a group of ragged wretches, men and women, gazing inside a rude bier, containing a corpse, whilst the wail of woman's voice sounded piteously from within. It was a fresh delicious morning, the sun just lighting the lofty mountain summits with a ruddy glow, and all external nature smiling with the enchantment of reviving life. These crimson glories of the dawn but saddened the gloom of the distant street, where death was couched with his victim, and the spirit of the pestilence, mantling over the stagnant ditches around, waited but the noonday heat to exhale its destructive breath. Some two miles from the gate, over the side of the causeway, lay the body of an Indian, but lately killed, the blood still oozing from a deep gash in the throat; whilst, ten miles farther on, in a field near the road, rose a newly-painted cross, with a fresh wreath of flowers pendent from its traverse. And thus does lawless vice and brutality heap their disfiguring monuments over this loveliest bijou of God's creative powers.

All attractions of interest to the traveller, between Mexico and Perote, have already been referred to; and, without an adventure on moor or mountain, inn or city, worth narration, I re-entered the courtyard of the meson of Perote, after an absence of nearly two months. This village, though containing a population of two thousand souls, and constantly filled with officers from the neighbouring fortress, is nearly as noted a haunt of brigands as Rio Frio itself. The houses are dark low-storied buildings, looking rather like so many forts than dwellings, and its inhabitants as piratical in appearance as they are reputed, and no doubt correctly, in practice. A few leagues to the east lies the Barranca Secca, a deep, gloomy, and wooded ravine, some half mile in length, through which the highway passes, picketed on either side by innumerable crosses. These significant monuments are each a separate record of some deed of blood and pillage, whose perpetrators have all, at one time or another, honoured Perote by their residence. With the exception of the filthy meson, supported by the coach passengers, and some dozen stores and shops, kept up by the patronage of the garrison, it has neither trade nor resources to maintain it, and the rest of its population live by ways and means, rather guessed at than avowed.

At as early an hour next day as warranted the application, I was at the castle gate, and after a short negotiation, was admitted to an interview with my unfortunate comrades. Two months of liberty, change of scene, pleasant rambles, and intercourse with kind friends, had mellowed, if not effaced from my mind, the stronger lines of that picture of captivity made up by their cruel sufferings and hardships, when we parted. Without knowing why, I had trusted to find their condition mitigated, their hopes revived, and their confinement but a humane security of their persons. Description would fail to elaborate the misery depicted in their emaciated appearance, and their desponding, hopeless looks and tones. I had left them loaded with calamities as heavily as I thought humanity could support, and was now surprised, as I heard their piteous tale, that nature and fortitude had not sunk overwhelmed under such burdens.

A more rigorous discipline and refined cruelty had been adopted toward them since I left, and such ingenious inhumanities inflicted on them, as to excite their surmises that the government had instructed the castle authorities to push them to some act of desperation as would justify their general massacre. Eleven of them were festering in the calaboose at the time of my arrival, for some trifling offence, loaded with twenty-five pounds of chains to each ankle; and Lieutenant Clopton, the most quiet and inoffensive of them all, was then in the hospital, not expected to live, from wounds inflicted on him because the rivet of his chain became loose. The same ruffian who committed this barbarous assault upon Clopton, about the same time had cruelly beaten and lamed a sickly and delicate boy, whom any government but Mexico would have deemed it foul shame to have retained a prisoner. Doctor Shepherd, a high-minded, brave gentleman, who had held the post of secretary of the navy of Texas, was assailed by two of these chivalric knights with drawn swords, for refusing to perform some degrading office, and only escaped by the courage and determination he evinced in resisting with his weaponless hands the offered indignity.

For more than a month their rations had been reduced to the lowest standard of supply, the little allowed them being musty rice and rotten potatoes, with meats so doubtful in character and repugnant in flavour, as to be only palatable to men reduced to the extremities of hunger.

In reply to their respectful remonstrances, the commandant taunted them with their cost and trouble to the government, and haughtily informed them that unlimited authority had been granted his subalterns for their control and government, and no farther complaints would be listened to against any officer of the garrison.

Such grievances as we have related, with a thousand other petty annoyances, added to the wholesale denial of all redress by the commandant, forced these wretched men, as a last alternative, to appeal to the British minister at Mexico against their inhuman oppression.

Their simple and eloquent memorial, transmitted to the capital after my departure, thus depicts their forlorn situation.

Castle of Perote, July 27th, 1844.
HIS EXCELLENCY CHARLES BANKHEAD:

Sir—The undersigned, a committee of all the prisoners now confined in the Castle of Perote, believing that we are abandoned by our government, have only the alternative left of appealing to the minister of Her Britannic Majesty at the court of Mexico, to interfere with a view of putting a termination to our sufferings and imprisonment. The evidences upon which our opinion is based, that we are surrendered by our government, are—

First, the letter to your predecessor, by the Executive of Texas, denouncing the Mier expedition as a lawless band of adventurers, unsanctioned by the authorities of the country from whence it came, and therefore unentitled to the consideration and protection which, by civilized usages and of right, belong to prisoners of war. Secondly, his withholding the means appropriated by Congress for our relief, when well apprised of our destitute and unfortunate situation.

Thirdly, his entire neglect to make any exertions in our behalf, either by way of mitigating our hard fate, or procuring our release. The only anxiety, within the knowledge of the undersigned, evinced by President Houston for the Texas prisoners, is to be found in the letter above referred to, which resulted in the melancholy tragic scene at the Ranch Salado, where were executed in cold blood seventeen as brave men as ever enlisted in the holy cause and under the sacred banner of liberty. Whether this solicitude was for our weal or wo, the probable tendency of its operation, and its actual lamentable consequences will show, not only to the satisfaction of those who executed, but those who promoted the horrid act. From this it will appear that this appeal properly emanates from the undersigned, and the sequel will show that it is appropriately addressed to your Excellency, the British minister. We believe, sir, that the government of Great Britain is under official obligation to demand our liberation. Under the auspices and through the avowed agency of the Charge d'Affaires of your government to Texas, a treaty for the mutual exchange of prisoners was entered into, and solemnly ratified by the contracting parties. Texas had confidence in this treaty, from the fact that your government became incidentally a party to it, your Charge d'Affaires having originated it.

She performed to the letter her obligations under it. The proclamation of President Houston not only gave full liberty to all the Mexican prisoners to depart the country, but offered them the means of taking them home, and an escort for their protection. But no corresponding act of good faith followed the fulfilment of her treaty stipulations by Texas. The undersigned and their comrades still suffer all the hardships of imprisonment. Their country has been entrapped and abused, and the Charge d'Affaires of Great Britain trifled with.

The undersigned do not rest their grounds for the interference of your Excellency in their behalf, upon the foregoing showing alone. They appeal to you and the whole corps diplomatique, as conservators of international law. Diplomatic agents clothed with ministerial powers, are called ministers to the different courts to which they are sent, which term, conjoined to their official duties, implies the possession of judicial authority. If this position be true, you are bound to notice all infractions of the great laws of nations, either in a state of peace or in the turmoils of war. It is your prerogative to control and regulate the operations of the latter state, when not conducted according to the principles of humanity, and the common mild usage of civilized nations. In the undersigned, and their unfortunate comrades, you have a case which solicits the controlling influence of foreign ministers. The humane maxims of international law, the acknowledged customs of civilized nations, have alike been violated and disregarded in our cruel treatment and unjust detention. When taken at Mier, under treaty stipulations guaranteeing to us safety and consideration, we were marched on foot through sunshine and through storm, and a portion of the way handcuffed in couples, under the taunt and lash of merciless Mexican soldiery. In the villages and towns through which we passed, instead of being treated with the kind courtesy usually extended by generous captors to vanquished enemies, we were received amid the hisses and maledictions of the infuriated rabble, with placards staring us in the face, commemorating the defeat of the Texan adventurers and robbers as we were termed.

The bloody tragedies enacted on the road, the undersigned refrain from recapitulating: their minds shrink with horror from the recital. Language is inadequate to express the deep agony of the heart in the bare review of such inhuman acts. Such has been our treatment on our way to Mexico, and the same harshness still continues. Only a few days since one of our men, (Lieutenant Clopton,) returned from the hospital in which he had been confined for five or six weeks, from the wounds and bruises inflicted upon him by a large bludgeon, in the hands of Captain Arroya, commandant of the castle. A few weeks ago a pale and sickly boy was so severely beaten by the same weapon, in the hands of the same officer, as to be compelled to carry his arm in a sling for some time. In a word, we are miserably fed, badly clothed, chained and worked like beasts of burden. Our hard fate is rendered yet more intolerable by the fact, that neither of the contending parties appear to make any active demonstration to bring the war to a close, but rather prefer becoming the clients of Great Britain, the United States, and France. The time necessary to render their mediation effective, must necessarily be long, and during this state of nominal peace, we have suffered, and still continue to suffer, all the hardships of an actual state of warfare.

Very respectfully,

F. M. GIBSON,	WILLIAM RYON,
CLAUDIUS BUSTER,	SAMUEL C. LYON.
WILLIAM S. FISHER,	*Committee.*

Since the above was written, they have all but one been liberated and returned to their homes. By whose agency, at whose appeal, or by what combination of circumstances and motives their emancipation was brought about, has not transpired. Mr. Navarro, a Mexican by birth, a federalist and foe to the military despotism that enslaved his country, alone remains in San Juan de Ulloa, having been condemned by the despot for his inexorable patriotism, to imprisonment for life.

So long as Santa Anna is at the head of the government, so long will this old and virtuous man partake of his fellest vengeance, to the bitter dregs. The coward who would instigate the assassination of the pure, the devoted, and learned Zavala, will not fail to wreak his relentless malignity upon so constant and courageous a friend of national independence as Navarro. Death, or the interposition of some intrepid and powerful champion of liberty and humanity, can alone rescue him from a speedy martyrdom.

Chapter XXVI

*Perote civility · The road · View
from Las Vigas · Beauty of Xalapa ·
Wagons and conductas · Puente Nacional ·
Tierra caliente · Litera · Manga de Clavo · Vera Cruz ·
Castle of Ulloa · Cutter Woodbury · Mr.
Dimond · Home.*

The whole plain of Perote was canopied with mist, obscuring the sides of the village streets from each other, as I took my early departure from the town. The ragged hostler of the meson pouched the gratuity for his nominal care of my half-starved horse, and bade me go somewhere, (other than the abode of the saints,) and a surly cur of the suburb, shut out by his night's ramble from his straw in the courtyard, volunteered his national antipathy on my exit, by snapping at my animal's heels several hundred yards along the road. Animal and human life are so intimately blended and impartially equalized in Perote, that these parting courtesies, though proceeding from different elements of their social composite, were but involuntary specimens of a uniform refinement.

Twelve miles on and the road springs from the flat and trenched plain up the rugged mountain acclivities, winding its way through moaning forests and mouldering crosses, whose omnipresent warning perpetually reminds the traveller in Mexico of the perils that surround him. To be reminded however, is not to be unnerved by the spectacle, for, notwithstanding the salutary consciousness of the insecurity of life and property these mementos inspire, their very profusion robs them of their terror, and but a few months' residence in the country is required to harden the most nervous against their gloomy forebodings.

Winding along the sides and up the defiles of the mountain, I at length reached the village of Las Vigas, perched on a lofty eminence, considered the highest point of the road between Mexico and Vera

Cruz. The mist which had been drifting from the eminences down upon the plain, was entirely dispelled at this point, and the sun breaking out with clear and dazzling brilliancy, lit up the scenery above with the utmost magnificence.

The peaks of Orizaba, the Cofre, and Tepicualca, jutted out from the vapour below, like glittering icebergs from the midst of the sea; whilst the snow-capped mountains on the distant horizon, half obscured by the intervening exhalations, looked like giant Titans whelmed to the shoulders in some surging inundation.

Passing through the villages of La Hoya and St. Michael, the road continues to descend, from sterility and desolation, along mountain spurs clothed with melancholy pines, until a sudden turn reveals the fairy and fruitful valley, out of which rises the picturesque city of Xalapa.

In the midst of a glen of perennial green, nodding with orange-trees, palms, groves of roses and acacias, rises a hill, whose terraced sides are covered to the summit with white-walled dwellings, temples, and convents. Around frown wild and fantastic mountains, whose shaggy sides are fringed with wilted pines and cedars, and bearded with aloes and agaves. The bloom and fragrance of the dell, and the romance of the adjacent scenery, are enhanced by the unrivalled taste, cleanliness, and luxury of the town itself. Selected for the beauty and salubrity of its site, it was built by the old Spanish merchants of Vera Cruz as a summer retreat for their families from the heat and pestilence of the sea-board. It numbers some ten thousand population, and is celebrated above all the cities of the republic for its intelligent society, and the marvellous beauty of its women. The streets are tortuous and steep, and the architecture massive and tasteful, the convent of San Francisco being amongst the largest and most ornamental monastic retreats in Mexico.

The extraordinary fecundity of the surrounding soil, and the humid yet genial climate it enjoys, overflow their market with fruits, melons, and vegetables, of every variety and excellence. Amongst these are peaches, cherimoyers, granadillas, pine-apples, oranges, guavas, and grapes, sold at prices that would scarce be deemed, in other lands, a recompense for gathering them.

East of Jalapa, the road continues over hills and heaths, with a gradual descent towards the coast, at one place sinking into ravines of goblin gloom, and at another bowling over ridges almost as level as the plain. In these elevated regions, the huts of its rude population are mostly constructed of hewn pine logs, floored and shingled after the fashion of our frontier cabins. So difficult and rugged is this mountainous way, that the teams of the diligence on this part are composed exclusively of patient and sure-footed mules, the hardy horses of the country being unequal to the task of drawing their heavy loads with safety.

Trains of American-built wagons, numbering fifty or seventy in procession, and drawn by twelve and sometimes fifteen mules, with caravans of *arieros* driving three and five hundred of these animals, loaded with merchandise for the interior, give an occasional aspect of commerce to these solitudes. But no other signs of life are to be met with, save here and there an isolated hovel, perched amongst the sterile hills, to denote an ownership for the straggling flocks that browse amongst their cliffs.

From the village of Plan del Rio, a series of short and easy slopes brings you to the Puente Nacional, a magnificent stone bridge that spans the precipitous banks of the river Antigua. A village of Indian huts, built of the bamboo cane, lies on one side of this mountain pass, and the ruins of fortifications on the adjacent heights show that its military importance has not been overlooked in former times.

After passing an undulating country of alternate plain and upland, decked with tropical trees and plants, but exhibiting at the same time a melancholy abandonment of inhabitants and cultivation, you enter sandy and extended forests, as primeval in their tangled and unviolated vegetation as they came from nature's hand. The rankness of the parasitic plants, festooning every branch of the enormous trees, and terracing their tops with beds of variegated bloom, the numerous stagnant and malarious-looking pools, hedged by banks of wild flowers, smiling like deceitful wreaths round poisoned goblets, the white-walled hacienda, and palm-thatched cottage of cane, proclaim you amongst the dangerous bowers of the *tierra caliente*.

Perched upon the summit of some blasted and creeper-covered tree sits the drowsy zapilote, snuffing the scented gale for some taint of his prey, whilst the ferocious destructor floats high in the empyrean above, watching the plain and mountain-side for a nobler banquet.

Beyond the little village of Manantial, I encountered, for the first time, a quaint but comfortable conveyance, not uncommon to the